The ROI Driv

Optimize Sales Performance
with an ROI Focused Sales Process

Steve Carson
David Connaughton

The ROI Driven Sale

ISBN 13: 978-1494859329
ISBN 10: 1494859327

Cover photo © Jim Brady http://jimbradyphoto.com/, used with kind permission.

This book is dedicated to our wives, June Carson and Marilyn Connaughton, and our families for their constant love and support throughout our active careers.

About the Authors

Steve Carson is founder and managing principal of Sales & Operations Advisors, LLC (www.salesopsadvisors.com), an innovative sales, marketing and operations consulting firm that helps software & technology companies improve sales and marketing performance and achieve revenue targets more effectively.

Prior to founding SOA, Steve was a member of the executive team of several leading and emerging software and technology companies where he was instrumental in improving go to market strategies, distribution channel development and market penetration resulting in significant sales and revenue growth. Several had exit strategies which concluded with highly lucrative results. He holds a B.S.B.A. degree from Bryant University.

David Connaughton is an international management consultant and business school adjunct professor with a long-running passion for operational excellence.

Prior to founding ROI-Team, David held advanced positions on IBM's financial team before performing and leading in-depth analyses for over 100 enterprises across the industry spectrum, from small start-ups to Fortune 100 companies. He is a graduate of the United States Air Force Academy and the Harvard Business School.

Acknowledgements

This book would not have been created without the encouragement and help of many friends and colleagues, including too many to name who provided inspiration and concepts over many years. In the production we were helped especially by our editor, Professor Neil Parmenter, and our proof readers, Shirley Poirier and Jane Goscewski. Any errors that remain after their fine work are ours alone.

Thanks also to Jim Brady, for creating the cover photo which we feel captures the excitement and precision of the winning ROI sales approach, and for the cover layout.

Using This Book

Sales Tips & Summaries

Many pages of this text include a very brief synopsis of the material, useful as a memory jogger for sales techniques and best practices.

Elevator Pitch

This summary box appears on some pages in Part 2 – with just enough information to convey in a one minute elevator ride with your prospect.

Step-by-Step

Some of the tools and techniques covered in Part 2 of this book benefit from an organized approach to execution. When called for, this step-by-step sidebar outlines that approach.

This book is intended as a reference for you, the salesperson or sales manager, offering a 'checklist' of steps to follow to initiate, develop, and close a sale incorporating financial content into the sales process.

The terminology used in this book is generally standard English, but recognizing that companies often have their own lexicon we have attempted to clarify terms that might be confusing with an extensive Glossary at the end of this book. In addition, since 'Sales' is the main topic, we describe customers and potential customers as follows:

- o Suspect: any entities that appear on a marketing list, generally comprised of target market organizations.
- o Lead: any suspect that is showing interest and may still require further nurturing and qualification of intent
- o Opportunity: a lead that has both interest and intent, making it 'qualified'
- o Prospect: an individual or an organization that appears ready to buy and represents a selling opportunity
- o Customer: a prospect that has purchased

The available CD- ROM by ROI-Team follows this text with illustrations, examples and ready-to-use tools in Excel format.

Available CD ROM Supplement

Many of the tools illustrated and described in this book can be obtained in ready-to-apply Microsoft Excel and PowerPoint formats on a CD from ROI-Team, Inc., at www.roi-team.us. Most are unprotected or protected without a password (the password entry field is left blank) so that you can modify them as needed.

In addition, the CD ROM contains PowerPoint slides summarizing the material, for reference or for training purposes. The available tools include:

01	ROI Sales Process	How do we execute the sales process?
02	Survey Instruments	What are our prospects thinking?
03	Base Case	How are they doing?
04	Current Metrics & Gaps	What should they measure?
05	Opportunity Chart	How does that affect their finances?
06	Value Proposition and Solution	What should they do?
07	Business Case	What is our solution worth to them?
08	Final Presentation – Excel forms	How do we construct and organize the charts?
09	Final Presentation – PowerPoint Slides	How do we put it all together?
10	Lean Six Sigma Tools	How do I discuss quality and efficiency with my prospects?
11 - 12	Chapter PowerPoint Slides	How can I train my sales team to use this ROI Driven process?

Contents

Introduction

ROI means Return on Investment, and specifically the financial return your prospective customers will experience after they invest in your product, service, or solution.

What worked selling costly enterprise solutions (software, equipment, process improvements, services, etc.) in the past is no longer effective in today's marketplace. Increasingly, educated buyers require a sophisticated, tailored approach – dramatically different from the feature-benefit and relationship-based approach of the past.

Companies need to build credibility and enthusiasm for their products and services before entering the sales cycle with effective web-based content that engages educated buyers / prospects as they seek solutions. Then the real work begins for the inside, direct, and outside partner sales team.

To win the business, the team must provide new ideas and a credible value-based business case that clearly outlines the Return on the Investment (ROI). As always, the team must have a sound knowledge of the buyers' needs, but it is also necessary to understand finance and especially ROI models in order to satisfy those needs. Together these key elements dramatically improve the sellers' ability to build an effective collaborative advisory relationship with the buyer and to communicate value across multiple levels of the organization.

This book describes the market development and sales processes that work best in today's marketplace, incorporating the critical ROI development that wins large sales.

Overview of Topics

THE OPTIMIZED COMBINATION OF

o Sales <u>operations practices</u> yielding
   EFFICIENCY,

o Sales <u>enablement skills</u> yielding
   EFFECTIVENESS,

and

o <u>Advisory skills</u> focused on new ideas,
   finance and value yielding
   TRUST

equals

THE ROI DRIVEN SALE

Sales Summary

The sales process has grown in complexity and intensity in today's highly competitive and quickly changing technology driven markets. Preparedness while following a few proven steps will greatly increase the probability of sales success.

The Steps to the ROI Driven Sale

For reasons of efficiency (avoiding duplicate or unnecessary work) and effectiveness (avoiding missing something important) it is useful to think through the steps in the sales process sequentially. Starting with the marketing groundwork that develops opportunities, and leads to a thorough development of relationships, understanding, idea generation, collaboration, financial impact, and a winning business case concluding with a satisfied customer, is illustrated here. The steps throughout the sales process and the financial knowledge it takes to execute with precision are all covered in this book.

PART 1: FOLLOW THE ROAD TO REVENUE

So you have a great product, service, or solution to offer at a competitive price. The sales process is lengthy and complex, but that's what it takes to offer ideas, build value, sell the ROI, and close the sales cycle. Now all you have to do is get noticed, demonstrate how your offering resolves important issues for potential customers and how your fit, features and benefits, value and ROI beat the competition. Right? Well…

Yours is a very common challenge in this era of changing technology, rising quality and falling prices. Business prospects are increasingly sophisticated and demanding. The chapters in Part 1 of this book provide a logically structured, step-by-step method of finding suspects, converting them to leads, nurturing them into opportunities, and then executing a winning sales process leading to a new customer win!

- o In today's highly competitive markets, there is a great deal to consider in preparing to sell your product or solution. Chapter 1 helps you get your arms around the key activities: developing a Go-To-Market strategy, creating messaging, determining your sales channel approach, managing your content, generating leads, managing the sales funnel, creating leadership buzz, and turning leads into opportunities.

- o Next, turning opportunities into customers takes both skilled salesmanship and proven processes and methods. Chapter 2 outlines a seven-step ROI Driven Sales Process that will increase your odds dramatically. The following chapters support the steps and incorporate time-tested techniques and concepts.

- o Chapter 3 discusses how to qualify the opportunity for interest and intent.

- Building trust and offering new ideas are critical factors in this process. People seldom buy from people they don't trust. <u>Chapter 4</u> describes what it takes to become a trusted advisor.

- You must propose a product or solution that your prospect will value more than the price you will charge. <u>Chapter 5</u> talks about how to create a compelling Value Proposition.

- Large, complex sales entail significant financial impacts, both positive and negative. In <u>Chapter 6</u> learn how to build a winning business case.

- This book is all about closing sales, the final step in the ROI-Driven Sales Process. <u>Chapter 7</u> offers proven ideas for ensuring that the sale gets closed and stays closed.

Embrace the process and gain the edge that will optimize your performance with proven best practices. Then review <u>Part 2</u> of the book for the business acumen and tools to execute the ROI Driven Sales Process to full effect.

Get Your Market in Order

Develop a Go-to-Market Strategy

Sales Tip

A GTM best practice is to first precisely identify the target market and then determine the right channel to reach it effectively and efficiently.

Selling a costly product or solution requires a carefully crafted Go-to-Market (GTM) strategy that specifies the approach to be used to deliver a unique value proposition to a target market. That value proposition is based on the choices the business has made, focusing on and investing in products and/or services which offer customers significant business benefits and a positive Return on Investment.

An organization's GTM strategy focuses on several questions, starting with the top 3:

- o   WHAT is the product or service (the SOLUTION) we are selling?
- o   WHO (what TARGET MARKET / DEMOGRAPHICS) will we sell it to?
- o   HOW (through what DISTRIBUTION CHANNEL) will we sell it?

These three questions spawn others – all critical to arriving at a winning GTM strategy – such as:

- o   HOW MUCH will we charge and what MARGIN should we plan?
- o   HOW will we promote (MARKET) it?
- o   WHERE (GEOGRAPHY) will we target our product sales?

These seem like common sense, yet many businesses struggle with Go-to-Market strategies and messaging that must be embraced and carried out effectively by the sales organization. When aligned properly, many benefits emerge including depth of market understanding, leadership positioning and consistent sales performance.

The key steps to create a GTM strategy, illustrated here, are:

1. Define the market value proposition / solution.
    a. What does the market need that you can offer?
    b. What can you sell your offering for?
    c. What does it cost your company to provide your product or solution?
2. Identify the primary target market.
    a. How big is it?
    b. How hard is it to reach?
3. Review market channel options.
    a. Which channels are best aligned with the target market?
    b. Will they be easy or difficult to work with?
4. Create a detailed channel approach.
    a. Based on answers to the previous questions, develop a complete road map to optimizing sales.

Analyze Target Markets and Develop Messaging

<table>
<tr><td>

Sales Tip

To get in the game, your message needs to resonate with challenges your target market faces. And don't underestimate the interest and credibility you can build with the web.

</td></tr>
</table>

Analyze the Market

Identifying the most appropriate target market is critical on numerous levels.

First, list all potential customers for your product or service. This will likely cross multiple industries, market segments and geographies.

Second, determine best fit characteristics such as size of prospective business in terms of revenue or number of employees, type of business, and also consider geography. This latter point will help you gain a clear understanding of where target market prospects are located and if there is an equal spread or if there are geographical pockets. This may have a bearing on your distribution approach.

Third, prioritize your market segments starting with those that are the best fit prospects based on need and fit with your solution. This segmentation will help the business think through all the possible target audiences for your solution and where to target based on best fit characteristics determined important.

Market narrowing allows for a more focused approach to all marketing and sales plans. Based on your Go-to-Market strategy and the target market, you are now well positioned to analyze and select your distribution channels. Verify that your selected target market and your desired sales channel match up. Ask yourself two questions:
1. Can the channel sell your product effectively?
2. Will your target buy from that channel?

Develop the Message

Messaging is the foundation for all marketing. An effective message strategy consists of a strong positioning statement and three to four support points addressing key target market problems. It starts by defining a compelling benefit

– why the target market should care about your product, service, company or technology. Understand that you are providing a need-satisfying solution.

The positioning statement is the central idea or theme for all your marketing messages. It is a short, declarative sentence that states just one benefit that addresses your target market's number one need. It needs to be unique, believable and in tune with your intended audience. Additional messaging builds upon the positioning statement to grab attention, build interest, establish credibility and demonstrate thought leadership. These elements move prospective clients closer to becoming interested buyers.

Messaging delivered via social and web marketing avenues has proven highly effective in building awareness, interest and credibility in advance of an actual sales cycle. This has been true especially during the past 5 years, and when combined with a more traditional public and media relations campaign can provide a holistic approach to developing target market opportunities.

Establish the Distribution Channel Mix

> **Sales Tip**
>
> Organize your channel strategy to create a WIN / WIN / WIN, for the customer, the channel, and you the vendor.

Many organizations start with a direct sales approach and evolve to use a mix of different channels. Selection and the mix need to be carefully tied to target markets being served and the product or service being sold.

There are several different channels from which to select:

o Direct – employee based sales organizations with direct (usually face to face) contact with prospective clients, typical in the sale of high value products or contracts to mid-sized and larger customers.

o Inside Sales – employee based sales organization usually with phone and web-based contact with prospective clients, typical in the sale of lower value products or small contracts, targeting mostly smaller and mid-sized companies; Social and web marketing and on-line presentations are heavily leveraged by this group.

o Reseller Partners – referral partners, resellers, Value-Added Resellers (VAR's). These third party organizations, although slightly different from each other, may sell their own product which is viewed as complimentary. Resellers usually cover a specific geographical territory and are focused on selling to smaller prospective clients, or to a specific market segment.

o Others – integrators, agents, franchises, and strategic alliances.

Every business has its own product mix, target markets, geographic emphasis, sales methodology, business strategy, revenue targets and budget, and all of these play key roles in determining the optimal mix. Careful planning is required to match business objectives, resources, and other infrastructure with the channels that make the most sense and to ensure that

marketing, channel management, and sales operations work in harmony to execute effectively and maximize the revenue opportunity.

A particularly efficient strategy with great Win/Win/Win potential is to partner with complementary resellers, who add value by combining your product with their own to offer a more attractive package. Everyone wins:

- The prospective client gets a more complete or personalized solution and more localized support.

- You the vendor get wider, more cost-effectiveness coverage with more prospective clients, improved profitability, and higher revenue generation.

- The reseller partner has an additional product portfolio to offer, to grow their customer base, sell more services, and increase revenue.

Especially when resellers (third-parties), are in the channel mix, the company needs to conduct on-boarding activities specifically designed to quickly and effectively make them productive, with some level of certification, so they can begin generating revenue. Dedicated resources are generally needed, dependent on the support model you structure. The support model will include responsibilities for training, certification, and mentoring, sales assistance, forecasting, monitoring quality, and assisting in the close of business. The company should monitor the performance over defined periods (monthly, quarterly, annually, etc.) and modify the channel accordingly to enhance performance.

Incentive planning and execution are always
key functions of sales management, and
each channel requires its own blend of rewards. For example, compensation for a reseller partner might be a much higher percentage than that for the inside or direct sales force, because resellers bear the cost of their own sales organization. The company can also provide sales support that makes it easier to sell, which can also affect sales compensation, and needs to consider the most cost-effective blend of incentives to customers and to salespersons in each channel. Typical actions that can be tailored to each channel include:

- Offering higher discounts to customers or commission percentages
- Premiums or special deals

- o Special considerations for trade shows
- o Allowances tied to advertising or branding activities.

The flip-side is also true, when negative actions may be necessary, such as shrinking assigned territory or reducing percentages or hold back delivery of product.

Channel conflict can arise when more than one party is involved in selling to the same prospective client or a division purchase in one location requiring corporate involvement in another location. Spell out the rules of engagement ahead of time, being specific about each situation to keep conflict to a minimum.

Key points to remember:

- o Clearly define territories and markets to minimize channel conflict
- o Ensure that rules of engagement are in place
- o Gain top management commitment on both sides of any selling relationship
- o Invest in partners to make it work – training, marketing, support
- o Communicate and collaborate constantly
- o Monitor performance – expect and inspect
- o Strive for Win/Win/Win

Effective Channel Management

Effective channel management requires…

- o Alignment with product or service solution offered
- o Well-thought-out support model
- o Frequent, effective training
- o Constant communications
- o Fair treatment – like your own sales force
- o Regular evaluation of adequately detailed performance metrics

Create a Sales Playbook

Sales Tip

Salespeople need ideas, facts, and figures at their fingertips to optimize their time with prospects. A well-thought-out playbook is a key tool to have in place.

What is a 'Sales Playbook?' Sales playbooks capture product information, application ideas, and best practices formatted for easy reference. They can help new salespeople during the on-boarding process, and are a key "go to" resource new and experienced sellers can leverage in real-time to ensure they are on track for top sales performance. What it ISN'T is a replacement for sales training.

Companies typically create a sales playbook to get salespeople to share and consistently leverage best practices. The objective is to make the selling process easy to follow and to leverage proven strengths and minimize demonstrated weaknesses.

Another key reason to create a sales playbook is to engage marketing and sales collaboratively in a systematic review of sales experience to identify proven best practices organized in a meaningful way that can be followed to yield increased efficiency, effectiveness, higher close ratios and improved revenue performance. This rigorous process benefits the company on numerous levels by thinking through where the best opportunities are, what impediments to sales success exist, and what resources and messaging is needed for both across the entire sales continuum.

Many companies operate without sales playbooks. That is not to suggest that the information doesn't exist, but rather is contained in a variety of documents used for other purposes, such as business plans, Go-to-Market strategy documents, sales plans, training materials, and product data sheets. Unfortunately for companies who do not operate with playbooks, the important information in those other documents may never be made available to the sales organization, or is poorly cobbled together for training purposes or worse yet left to the salesperson to figure out.

Most likely, some but not all of the material that can go into your sales playbooks already exists somewhere in your company. Prioritized segments, target prospects, competitive differentiators, buyer roles, win strategy, and even the sales process may be contained in the marketing plan or sales training material. Companies using a content management system may be well positioned to direct salespeople to sales enablement content (call scripts, email templates, success stories, case studies, analyst reports, etc.) which may be further organized based on prospect role, need and phase of the sales process. Some companies subscribing to a sales methodology have paper cue worksheets or the equivalent built into their CRMs that walk salespeople through qualifying prospects, probing for key needs and desired capabilities, as well as quantifying the impact the new solution could have. These systems organize key messages by role, segment, and need.

Some organizations with very experienced salespeople opt for short sales playbooks that simply highlight how their key markets differ in pains, capabilities needed, and the perceived benefits the solution could help them achieve. Other organizations have produced sales playbooks covering each stage of the sales process in detail.

Sales playbooks are unique to each business and need to be customized to fit a company's specific product, market and situation. A sales playbook for a company selling $5K solutions over the phone will be very different from one for companies selling $250K solutions or for those selling $1M+ solutions in complex RFP situations. Here are three examples to illustrate different playbook concepts:

1. Short Sales Cycles, Low Solution Prices: The sales playbook for a company selling a low-priced solution may be via an outbound email or telemarketing campaign targeted at a specific customer segment. The playbook may outline the entire sales process from initial prospect engagement through close. It might include an email campaign, mailings, phone scripts to follow-up on, calls to action such as case studies or analyst reports, and quick reference sheets on competitors. Usually dictated by price, the solution in this case requires high activity and high volume touches, warranting a highly scripted playbook.

2. Longer Sales Cycles, Higher Solution Prices: At the other end of the spectrum, salespeople selling higher-priced, more complex solutions

generally follow a less scripted sequence. A salesperson in situations like this might normally have phases to their sales process, such as:

I. Company and departmental research
II. Networking in target companies
III. Confirmation of need associated with your solution
IV. Consideration stage (often a lengthy phase – see Chapter 2, 'Build Sales Momentum…').

A sales playbook for this type of salesperson might include:

o A guide for what data to gather in the research stage
o Messaging scripts by prospect type (role) which outlines prospect's pain, solution capability and benefit to prospect - Email and phone
o Thought leadership materials to build advisory relationship with executives
o Qualification questions
o Product features and data sheets
o Materials which establish Company credentials
o Customer case studies and success stories
o Competitive info including how to compete strategies (understanding strengths and weaknesses)
o How to overcome key objections
o A financial metrics guide to help salespeople quantify (with prospect participation and buy-in) the potential impact of the solution (these are key for the ROI and business case development – see Chapter 4, 'Determine the Impact').

There could also be a section on key sales process insights. For example, if multiple business units within a prospect could use a solution, this insights section might advise on which line of business is likely to benefit the most in order to locate the most willing champion or sponsor. Or if there are executives who will be threatened by the change, there might be advice on how to neutralize their opposition.

3. New Solution, or New Market: Most companies don't develop a sales playbook for new market segments or solutions until pioneering salespeople report back what works and what doesn't. When you first enter a new market or are rolling out a new product, you have hypotheses for which customer needs your solution addresses, what messages will

resonate, and what the sales process should be, but you need to Build and frequently modify initial premises. If you want to lay out your premises in a formal document, build a lightweight sales playbook summarizing these assumptions and be prepared to modify these early and often as new information comes in.

For situations outlined in the complex or new markets described in steps 2 and 3 above, there is a large amount of information to be absorbed by salespeople. The Playbook Snapshot card is a tool used by many sales organizations to present highlights of the items described to facilitate the proper messaging, solution value drivers, appreciation for the buyers' needs, understanding of the financial impact, and so on, while executing the prescribed best practices in the course of the sales cycle. Make it intuitive and accessible. Boil down the high value 'best practices' and associated messaging and get them into a quick-reference medium such as a tablet or multi-fold laminated card.

> ### Sales Tip
>
> An effective sales playbook offers key selling ideas covering a variety of customer, industry, and solution-related topics in an easy-to-use format.

Generate Leads

> ### Sales Tip
>
> Lead generation methods are rapidly evolving in cost and effectiveness. Make the right choices by leveraging Search Engine Optimization (SEO) to gain visibility and market-specific content to surface sales leads.

Lead generation activity choices are like an alphabet soup: advertising, web, mail, phone, events, webinars, workshops, Public Relations, media, social networking, customer references, telemarketing, trade shows, industry associations, leadership forums, product reviews, print, digital, enterprise content management, and speaking engagements. Topping the list are lead generating activities associated with the web and digital content..

How do you generate leads for your business? How effective is it? Until recently, the concept of "lead generation" meant marketing found the names of potential buyers and passed them to sales. Buyers expected that they would have to talk to sales and sales expected to speak to early stage buyers that may not be qualified and may have limited familiarity with your product category.

This has all changed. Today's buyers do their own research using search engines, social media, and other online channels, and can learn a great deal about a product or service before ever speaking to a sales person. They often decide whether to even consider a product based on the abundance of information readily available online. Reaching these 'self-directed buyers' requires new techniques to develop and qualify potential leads, starting with an effective digital presence. Every organization needs to analyze its lead generation effectiveness continuously and adapt its initiatives accordingly.

Have you tried multiple approaches to generate leads? If you want to reinforce your message to be heard above the noise in the market, and/or if you serve multiple market segments, the answer needs to be 'yes.' And your methods need to be increasingly creative. Instead of finding customers with mass advertising and email blasts, marketers must now focus on being found on the web and learn to:

1. Develop content that resonates with their target markets
2. Build continuous relationships with buyers
3. Be viewed as a Trusted Advisor that can offer new ideas
4. Show the value with impactful ROI cases

Work the Web

> ### Sales Tip
>
> A solid web-based lead generation strategy can help capture the interest of your buyer and demonstrate thought leadership before they are even ready to contact sales.

With the growth of the internet, the world has changed from one of information scarcity to one of information abundance. The problem is that information abundance equals attention scarcity. This is known as attention economics and has transformed the buying process. Buyers are overwhelmed with all the noise and they are getting better and better at ignoring the messages they don't want to hear and researching what they do want to learn about on their own.

Clearly, there has been a huge change in the traditional buying process. In fact, according to Forrester, buyers might be anywhere from two-thirds to 90% of the way through their buying journey before they even reach the vendor. The reason this is happening more and more is because buyers have so much access to information that they can delay talking to sales people until they are practically experts themselves.

In this environment, you don't want your sales team spending time going down a list and cold calling if you can gain attention, generate leads and convert them to revenue faster. And how do you do this? Become a trusted advisor to your prospects by creating and publishing valuable content assets and thought leadership.

Manage the Sales Funnel

Many marketing departments are allocating more budget to the most effective lead generation tactics – company websites, conferences and trade shows, email marketing and Search Engine Optimization (SEO). (Direct mail and print ads are least effective, according to IDG.) The inbound marketing spend in particular has been growing as companies need to find more creative ways to break through the noise and get leads into the sales funnel.

With the new type of buyer it is important to note that marketing efforts don't end once a new lead comes into the system – known as Top of the Funnel (TOFU) marketing. Many companies do a good job at generating leads, but the problem is that most new leads are not ready to purchase. And if a sales person, inside or outside, does engage and the lead isn't ready to talk with him or her, it reinforces the notion that marketing sourced leads are of low quality. As a result leads get lost, ignored, or snatched up by competitors.

First Contact
Web, Social Media, Industry Groups, Trade Shows, Mailings, Etc.

Nurturing
Phone Calls, Meetings, Webinars, Success Stories

Active Sales Cycle
Value Proposition, Solution, ROI / Business Case

Close

$

To prevent this, good marketers invest in lead nurturing and other Middle of the Funnel (MOFU) techniques to build relationships and trust – earning the lead's business once he or she is finally ready to buy. This holistic strategy focuses on getting the timing right and engaging leads with relevant content.

Sales Tip

Sales-readiness as ranked by lead scoring is key to determining the handoff timing between Marketing (nurturing) and Sales.

Marketing and Sales alignment is critical to optimizing the performance of all revenue generating initiatives including lead generation practices, and keeping score is key. Lead scoring is a shared sales and marketing method for ranking leads in order to determine their sales-readiness. Leads are scored based on the interest they show in your business, their position in the buying cycle, the potential revenue they represent and their fit with offered products and services. Scoring helps companies know whether prospects need to be fast-tracked to sales or developed with lead nurturing. The best marketing programs have intentional measurement strategies planned in advance, answering these questions:

- o   What will we measure?
- o   When will we measure?
- o   How will we measure?

Create Leadership Buzz

It sounds personal, and is in fact a personal leadership skill as well as a company objective. Individuals and businesses that can effectively communicate expertise as leaders and create "buzz" are well positioned to develop relationships as trusted advisors and build a loyal following for the business solution they offer.

Unfortunately, there is no handbook or framework to guide sales individuals in developing executive presence and becoming a leader and a trusted advisor. Generally speaking, there are four characteristics most crucial to executive presence necessary to create leadership buzz:

1. Demeanor – the largest portion of communication is non-verbal: facial expression, eye contact, and projection of inner confidence. The right dress, hygiene, posture and demeanor convey a professional, executive image.
2. Communicate Insight – speak the business language important to your prospective customers and educate them with new ideas and perspectives, while connecting your ideas with their business strategy.
3. Personalize – connect with those you're speaking to by adapting your style and developing rapport with them. Actively listen and be open to other points of view.
4. Results – work to develop a reputation as one who gets results, is a thought leader, and goes above and beyond to get the job done. Spark new thinking, and stir passion.

> ## Sales Tip
>
> Thought leadership and innovative ideas can lead to becoming a trusted advisor. When companies do it, they improve their chances of reaching the industry top quadrant. When individuals do it, they increase their credentials with prospects and improve their win performance.

Don't make the mistake of thinking that simply doing a good job and getting results will create leadership buzz. Proactively enhance your development of these skills by seeking honest feedback from a mentor. Ask him or her, what you most need to improve. Then practice developing those skills in meetings, conference calls, and even in your email correspondence. And remember to always be intentional about the impression you are leaving with others. It is very much like establishing your own personal brand, the image you will use to advance your skills in building leadership buzz and becoming a trusted advisor. So...

1. Identify key concepts or ideas you firmly believe in and have strong knowledge about. It may be the business value your solution yields (i.e., value proposition, ROI, etc.). Become an expert on it.
2. Continually educate yourself on the identified topic, so you are effective in leading discussions and providing associated new ideas. Listen to other leaders in the field, gain new perspectives and obtain feedback from others you respect about your ability to communicate your ideas at leadership levels.
3. Socialize. Your ability to discuss your ideas shows up in many different work situations: meetings, phone calls, emails, business presentations, industry trade groups, etc. Look for opportunities where you can socialize your ideas. Start small, with one-on-one meetings and then consider expanding it to speaking engagements or social writing (blogs, etc.) that enable you to further develop and expand your leadership ideation.

Convert Suspects to Leads

The 'how to' of developing a strong sales funnel starts with getting marketing and sales on the same page with the appropriate steps to find, develop, and convert suspects to qualified prospects. If you haven't yet developed a lead management system, that is the best place to start. Collaboratively establish agreed-upon definitions of process steps leading to a 'qualified lead' (referred to as an 'opportunity' in this book).

> ### Sales Tip
>
> The impact of a 'fit-first' approach is enormous. In many organizations, 50% of sales energy is spent on prospects who never convert.

Then establish a lead nurturing system for all the suspects and leads so sales can get the opportunities they want and marketing can get the recognition they deserve. Your process will systematically take your suspects and nurture them over time into interested prospects (leads), and ultimately turning them into opportunities. Here are a few ways you can simplify and automate your suspect to lead to opportunity management efforts:

1. Know your ideal prospective customer 'profile fit'
2. Define and agree on lead stages and lead terminology
3. Understand the difference between interest and intent
4. Give your leads a score and a grade
5. Stay top of mind with non-sales-ready leads, be visible
6. Create engaging, supporting content
7. Be viewed as a trusted advisor
    a. at a company level
    b. at a sales rep level
8. Create opportunities that generate revenue.

The initial steps in this process help minimize the noise by eliminating non-fits and distinguishing suspects from leads and leads from opportunities.
By the time you reach items 5-7 above you need to be ready with effective content, which will grow over time and will become a key resource for your business development initiatives.

Manage the Content

The beauty of content development is that almost everyone in your organization can be involved. Senior Management, Sales, Marketing, Services, Development, Operations, and Support all have areas of expertise worthy of communicating to your target market audience. Content will include: case studies, success stories, presentations, blogs, webinars, trade show, industry events, speaking engagements, research reports, and the list goes on. Each plays a role in building company and individual credentials. This is your way of showing your universe of target market prospects that you are the experts that can lead them to new ideas which will become competitive advantages for them.

Having content is only part of the process. At least as important is getting it into the right hands. How do you make that happen, and become more visible to your universe of prospects? The marketing organization will be the main driver for the establishment, development and maintenance of the Content Management System (CMS). For most companies, this will be housed electronically in a digital repository that is an integral part of the company website. This CMS helps with content organization, management, delivery, and monitoring and analytics that become critical to the staged development of the sales funnel. It is also instrumental in on-boarding new employees and scaling the business with consistent messaging. Creating the buzz and spreading the word has changed in many ways during the past 5 years.

   o   Search Engine Optimization (SEO) helps your site and content become more visible. Pay per click and Google Ad words can be effective contributors to advancing message pick up percentages.
   o   Public Relations and media relations are also very important in circulating your stories and messages to influencers who can make a difference in your product visibility. PR and Media relations has shifted in many ways away from print and advertising to electronic forms of social media (twitter, Facebook, LinkedIn, etc.) and blog posts.

Leverage the Content

Becoming a trusted advisor as a company and as an individual sales person, with support from the Content Management System, has a significant impact on the ability to close sales. This can be accomplished in a two-pronged process:

1. The <u>company</u> becomes highly visible via its web presence, its reviews by analysts, its participation in industry groups as speakers and panelists and its constant flow of new content (case studies, success stories, etc.) in which the company displays new insights on driving further value for its customers. Growth of its customer base further extends its credentials.
2. In addition to the company credentials directly impacting the <u>individual sales person</u> in his/her ability to be taken more seriously by the prospective customers, the individual sales person can also have a direct impact by:

    a. Taking on activity in industry settings attended by prospective customers, such as a speaker or panelist, or by facilitating a speaking engagement highlighting one or more customers.
    b. Building questioning skills when gathering and interacting with prospective customers, allowing the salesperson to add value by offering new insights and bring confirming or challenging thoughts to the discussion. The salesperson is no longer seen as selling products but as focused on providing solutions to problems.
    c. Enlightening the prospective buyer with value propositions and an understanding of the financial aspects of the business, and relating it to the expected ROI.

Facilitating discussion with the right questioning inquiry techniques can be very effective in achieving improved interactions with prospects. Appreciating the buyer's business challenges and having ideas to share in a non-threatening manner can change a buyer's perspective of what's possible and create a better chance of influencing his or her agenda. Questions might include:

1. 'Why' questions. – i.e., "Why is that your Plan?"
   Do not put the prospect on the defensive. The tone of must be collaborative, not judgmental.
2. 'How questions'? – i.e., "How do you see this working?"
   These help people think about reality, very helpful in generating insights.

3. 'Have you considered' questions? – i.e., "Have you considered options A, B, C?"
    They may not have thought about other options, which can be further explored.
4. 'What will the impact be with or without' questions.
    The response will provide insights into how you can help the prospect decide – and buy.

Turn Leads into Opportunities

Too many marketing organizations toss leads over the wall to the sales force, wasting the time of one of the organization's indispensable resources, the people who bring in the revenue. To convert a lead to an opportunity requires close collaboration between marketers and salespeople. Before the hand-off, marketers need to ensure that the lead…

- Has needs that your products and services fill
- Has money

And ensure that your sales force…

- Has every scrap of knowledge the marketing department has to offer about
  - The prospect and the prospect's industry
  - The key contacts
  - Any history or current issues to resolve with the prospect
  - The suggested solutions to offer
- Has the tools and training to follow the Seven-Step Sales Process to its conclusion, a profitable sale.

Once a lead has become an opportunity, it's time for the salesperson to swing into action.

Develop Sales Momentum with the ROI Driven Sales Process: Qualify, Build, Close (QBC)

Sales Tip

The 'ROI-Driven Sale' is a guided process that confirms interest and intent, builds advisory trust, connects the business dots and paints a picture of the new reality with a business case showing high impact monetized value and ROI yielding a timely call to action.

After nurturing a prospective buyer, the marketing team has provided you, the salesperson, with a qualified lead they categorize as an 'opportunity.' You are equipped with professional skills, knowledge of your prospects industry and business, product messaging that will resonate with the prospect, and a fluent understanding of the functional and business benefits your prospect will derive based on the use of your product. You also have the necessary financial acumen (covered later in this book) to build an effective business case with compelling ROI.

The process described in the next several chapters is also outlined in the 'ROI Sales Checklist' in this chapter and, in case you want to modify it, on the available CD ROM toolkit.

Let's get started on the ROI-Driven road to success!

.

ROI Driven Sales Flow

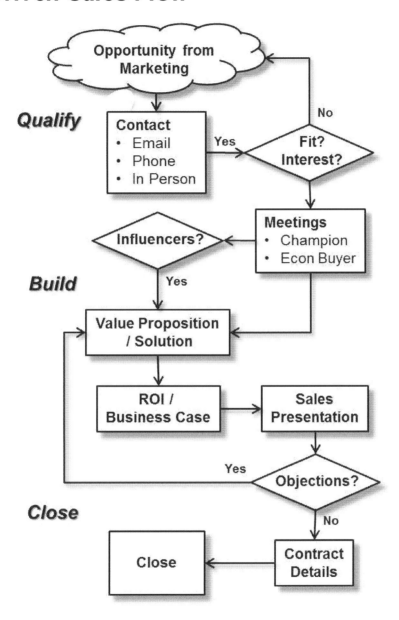

ROI Driven Sales Checklist

Sales Activities (Once a Lead Has Become an Opportunity)	√
Investigate Goals, Challenges, and Strategic Importance (5 W's)	
WHO are the 'Big Three' players?	
WHAT are the challenges, Value-Proposition, ROI and the Project or Initiative?	
WHY will each of the key players want to buy?	
WHERE is the money source?	
WHEN is the project kickoff desired?	
QUALIFY for Interest and Intent	
Step 1 — Make the initial prospect call and qualify the interest	
Step 2 — Meet in person and continue to develop the opportunity and confirm the intent	
BUILD Interest, Offer Ideas, and Establish the Value and ROI	
Step 3 — Explore prospects goals, challenges and desires, while showing prospect you understand their business	
Continue to develop interest using success stories, and best practices research and collaborative discussions with Champion	
Prioritize key business drivers meeting business goals	
Offer innovative ideas and insights and personalize them Collect key financial data and determine metrics that matter	
Expand and develop relationships to include EB and other influencers in addition to Champion	
Conduct preliminary product demonstration (if warranted)	
Assess your trusted advisor status	
Create and Test the Value Proposition, Develop the Business Case and ROI	
Step 4 — Take collected financial data, measure gaps, employ opportunity charts	
Calculate ALL costs, determine financial benefits	
Build Value Propositions around prioritized business drivers	
Calculate the TOTAL Return on Investment (ROI) Identify any and All risks associated with obtaining ROI	
Create a financial and non-financial business case narrative	
Present preliminary Value Propositions, Business Case and ROI with Champion and Economic Buyer, collaborate on any changes and confirm intent to move forward	

	Prioritize agenda topics for Product presentation/demonstration	
	Set-up call between EB and your Company executive to connect seller and buyer at senior levels (VP, CXO)	
	Call will reinforce your Company's credentials, interest in a long term relationship and key Value Prop benefits identified	
	During call, look for confirmation from EB of Value, intent to move forward and EB's plan to be an integral part of a group demonstration / presentation	
Present the Winning Business Case		
Step 5	Proactively manage the intended audience and balance of power	
	Open with Value Proposition presentation outlining the prioritized challenges, desires and monetized value	
	Demonstrate the product / solution, during which, reinforce where and how the ROI will be achieved. Throughout get confirming buy-in from the group. Summarize value and review high level deployment plan	
	Meet separately with EB and Champion review proposal and contracts	
	Verify approval steps necessary for final contract sign-off	
CLOSE the SALE - Get to 'Yes,' Map the Gates, and Drive the Timelines		
Step 6	Plan post-demonstration meetings to maintain momentum	
	Verify that the approval process is moving forward and handle any objections	
	Review each step of the approval process	
	Schedule short interval follow-ups to keep the process moving	
	Reinforce the ROI, Value Props and Business Case with Champion and EB	
	Work through any Terms and Conditions (T's & C's) adjustments with legal	
Step 7	Maintain constant contact with the Champion and EB as they run interference with their internal approval process	
	Keep them fluent with the ROI and business benefits as they are your buyers internal sales organization for the moment	
	Negotiate the final contract and close	
Follow up with great customer service as though your next sale depended on it		

Qualify the Opportunity

Investigate Goals, Challenges, and Strategic Importance

The Seven-Step ROI Driven Sales Process begins with a thorough understanding of the opportunity by researching, understanding and developing the '5 W's':

- o WHO are the 'Big Three' players:
    - o Champion
    - o Economic Buyer
    - o Endorser/s
    - o And who are influencers?
- o WHAT are:
    - o The challenges (pain) / desires (gain)
    - o The Value-Proposition
    - o The Project or Initiative and its ROI?
- o WHY will each of the key players want to buy? Is the need or project important? How does it impact the business relative to revenue, expense, and /or market-position?
- o WHERE is the money source (corporate, division, budgeted, discretionary)?
- o WHEN is the project kickoff desired? What is the close timeline (identify milestones and gates)?

This research should be done as thoroughly as possible before the first contact. Then:

Step 1:
Make the initial call (by phone or in person) to qualify the prospect with respect to the level of interest. The goal of this call is to confirm interest, develop further momentum, and set up next steps with key influencers and the Economic Buyer.

Step 2:
Meet in person and continue to develop the opportunity, with more specific insights into the prospect's goals, challenges and readiness for further exploration. Continue to validate the intent and build interest with the EB.

In addition to confirming the opportunity and developing interest during these first two steps, it is important to identify and meet with the Champion (the key business sponsor), and separately with the Economic Buyer (the person who owns the budget). Use prepared business case development materials and lead discussions to further confirm and define the opportunity.

With the Champion:
- o Develop a relationship, build rapport
- o Ask the '5 W's' to understand the overall state of the business
- o Gain an understanding of key company initiatives and challenges
- o Develop an initial value proposition
- o Gage the Champion's and the organization's enthusiasm
- o Identify the Economic Buyer (EB) and find out…
  - o How long he / she has been with the company
  - o His / her relationship with the Champion
  - o What his/her priorities are
- o Set-up for a meeting with EB.

With the Economic Buyer:
- o Discuss the need – pain, gain, interest, and priorities
- o Test and expand the value proposition and ROI objectives
- o Determine personal wins
- o Confirm the Champion's strength in organization
- o Ask about other key players or influencers whose support is needed in the decision making process

With influencers (as confirmed by EB):
- o Review business case materials
- o Gain interest and support
- o Map the people who influence the sale – power individuals, strengths and weaknesses, friends and foes

> ## Sales Tip
>
> During the Qualification stage, strive to keep your meeting sizes small, ideally 1 to1. This will enable more rapport and relationship building opportunities with your Champion and other key players. Do not lose the Balance-of-Power by being dramatically out-numbered.

Build Trust and Offer New Ideas

Be a Credible Business Problem Solver and Trusted Advisor

Building trust and offering new ideas are critically important to selling when long sales cycles and substantial monetary investments are required. In most cases you must establish yourself as a credible and trustworthy expert before the business ideas you have to offer will be taken seriously. A trusted advisor:

Sales Tip

To become a trusted advisor, you must:
- Be an active listener
- Establish credibility through ability to offer new and innovative ideas
- Be highly reliable – quick to respond and thorough
- Balance asking questions with giving advice
- Collaborate with prospective customer with long term view
- Offer new ideas
- Demonstrate that you are investing your time in their success.

- Puts the prospective customer's interests before his / her own and is genuinely interested in helping a prospective customer's business
- Works hard to understand a prospective customer's business challenges and desires in detail prior to ever trying to offer a solution
- Is credible based on the educational value of ideas offered and / or proven relevant previous customer successes
- Connects with the prospect both constructively and emotionally by demonstrating keen business insights tied to the future upside (ROI) and downside risks (loss of competitive edge) with and without the solution
- Is reliable and consistent, as measured by speed and thoroughness in all follow-ups
- Is authentic, while being passionate and enthusiastic about his / her solution advice

- o   Treats the business relationship as if it will be long term
- o   Recognizes that building trust takes time and requires dedicated work

Your prospect cares more about the monetized business value (ROI) and the personal benefit (career enhancement, visibility, improved performance, etc.) your product / solution will provide than about its pure productivity or efficiency benefits. To bring new ideas that get attention, you must be highly educated on your prospective customer's industry and business so as to be able to contrast and compare impactful business data such as:

- o   Best practices
- o   Industry benchmarks
- o   Research / White papers
- o   Videos, webinars

Then you need to personalize your delivery of insights by describing how they impact the prospect, offer your ideas in an educational and collaborative manner, and show results and deployment scenarios as proof statements which generate additional ideas and establish credibility simultaneously.

Businesses large and small are faced with complex, open-ended, ever-changing challenges (and desires) and realize that ongoing innovation is critical to staying ahead of the competition. Be on the lookout for new ideas that can drive innovation and spark creativity, a differentiating skill that you can cultivate.

We often make the mistake of assuming that good ideas just happen, or that creativity is an aptitude that some people have and others don't, or that we are not intelligent enough to come up with good ideas. These assumptions are rarely true. You can come up with fresh, radical ideas – you just need to learn to open your mind to forge new connections, think differently and consider new perspectives.

This creativity starts with rich knowledge of the area you are working on. Prepare yourself with adequate information about the challenges and desires your solution typically satisfies in the industry setting you are selling into.

Once you have deep background knowledge, you need to avoid getting stuck in unproductive thought patterns. Breakthroughs occur when you:

- o <u>Challenge assumptions</u>: For every situation, you have a set of key assumptions. Challenging these assumptions gives you a whole new spin on possibilities.
- o <u>Reword the problem</u>: Stating the problem differently often leads to different ideas. To reword the problem look at the issue from different angles. Ask:
    - o "Why do we need to solve the problem?"
    - o "What's the roadblock here?"
    - o "What will happen if we don't solve the problem?"

    Questions such as these often provide new insights and lead to unexpected and effective new solutions
- o <u>Reverse the thinking</u>: If you feel you cannot think of anything new, try turning things upside-down. Instead of focusing on how you could solve a problem, improve operations, or enhance a product, consider how you could create the problem, worsen operations, or downgrade the product. The resulting ideas, when reversed, may be possible solutions for the original challenge.
- o <u>Look for ideas in different media</u>: When faced with workplace challenges we tend to rely on verbal reasoning. Consider the challenge through different media (visualization, anecdotes, success stories, webinars, etc.).
- o <u>Seek possible ideas from unexpected places</u>: Look for solutions to similar problems in other industries or situations. Ask questions such as:
    - o "What are the functions needed to solve this problem, and what functional equivalents are available ANYWHERE?"
    - o "What attributes of this item could help us solve our challenge?"
- o <u>Get other perspectives</u>: Collaborate with as many influencers as feasible and ask each what they would do if faced with your challenge. Approach

others engaged in a different kind of work who might see things differently.

o <u>Play the "what if" game</u>: Ask yourself "What if I were ... How would I address this challenge?" Imagine yourself to be anyone: CEO, industry trade organization head, a millionaire, anyone. The idea is the person you decide to be has certain identifiable traits, and you must use these traits to address the challenge. For instance, if you decide to play the millionaire, you might want to bring traits such as flamboyance, big thinking and risk-taking when formulating an idea. If you are CEO you would focus on things such as financial performance, customer satisfaction, and execution detail.

Building trust combined with offering new ideas will make you a trusted advisor and can increase your sales performance dramatically

Establish the Value Proposition

It is easy to get the attention of your prospects if the solutions you offer provide huge, impactful benefits for problems looming large on their radar. It behooves you to learn as early as possible just how important your solution will be. The next steps in the process, incorporating the generally iterative ROI development process of Chapter 6, 'Determine the Impact,' lead up to the closing. During these steps the objectives are to connect the challenges and desires with functional benefits of the solution and to Build and quantify the ROI.

> ## Sales Tip
>
> Add strength to the value proposition by expressing the compelling value and benefits from the prospect's personal (career enhancing) and business (operating benefits) perspective.

Step 3:

Survey prospects to understand the customer requirements in order to define the value proposition. This step often provides opportunities to introduce new ideas and educate the prospect about new solutions and evolving cost-benefit considerations. Activities include:

o   The Champion prioritizes the drivers yielding largest business benefit
o   Interviews and surveys are conducted with all key influencers to confirm current processes and quantify impact with new solution
o   Further probing of business requirements takes place to ensure all potential needs are identified and mapped to solution capabilities, driving value propositions and projected monetized value
o   Gain enough input to prioritize the product demonstration
o   Financial information collected to formalize Value Proposition Document and Return on Investment Document

Build the Winning Business Case

Step 4:

Using the survey results and other collected data, build a variety of value propositions, ROI models and business scenarios using the sections in this chapter. These will comprise much of the business content to be presented to the Champion and Economic Buyer (EB) prior to the demonstration / final presentation. This chapter of the book will help you build a Winning Business Case.

Once you have completed the business case, you will be ready for...

Step 4b:

Preview the solution and business case with the Champion and, when he or she is on board, with the Economic Buyer. NEVER go into a final sales presentation without knowing exactly where each key decision-maker stands. Activities include:

- Set up a call between the EB and your company executive to connect seller and buyer at senior levels
- Your company executive...
    - Reinforces your company's credentials and interest in a long term relationship with the EB's company
    - Re-states at a high level the key value proposition benefits that have been identified
    - Looks for confirmation from the EB of the value and the intent to move forward
    - Ensures there are no surprises in store
- You or your company executive invite and encourage the EB to be an integral part of the final presentation and ask for time afterward to review any questions

Determine the Metrics that Matter

Sales Tip

Find out what your prospect values most and focus on accurately measuring the current state to develop a credible baseline.

Step-by-Step

1. Review the metrics the prospect uses
2. Review year-on-year performance
3. Review industry benchmarks for cost ratios (per cent of revenue by category)
4. Develop new ratios that link your solution to prospect performance (see the Chapters on Metrics and Financial Literacy in this book for ideas)

A Business Case estimates the impact – especially financial – supporting any investment, such as equipment or software installations, business acquisitions, focused Six Sigma projects, broad Lean Production Culture projects, or any other initiatives aimed at improving business results.

Improvements are likely to impact your prospects' finances in one of four positive ways:

○ Increased revenue
○ Decreased Cost of Goods Sold
○ Decreased corporate overhead
○ Decreased asset requirements (with associated period expenses such as depreciation and carrying costs)

These benefits will be offset by investments in:

○ Added corporate overhead spending (on people who do the work, for instance)
○ Added assets (machinery, equipment, software and the like) with associated period expenses such as depreciation and carrying costs)

The Business Case starts with an accurate view of the current baseline in areas that your solution addresses. The metrics that define this baseline might include (to the level of granularity required, by category or department):

- Current revenues generated
- Current operating costs and efficiency ratios
- Current asset requirements and efficiency ratios
- Current headcount applied
- Any other current income, expense, assets, or resources that your solution might impact

The metrics selected need to both excite the client and link logically to the solution you offer. For example, software solutions often ease the administrative workload and allow reduction or reassignment of staff members, or might increase revenue by improving sales force efficiency, or reduce inventories by making them more visible or easier to distribute. Selling your solution is dramatically easier when these are red issues to the prospect.

Measure the Gaps

Sales Tip

Establish the 'Base Case' and keep the sales efforts focused on areas where the money is.

Step-by-Step

1. Collect and review P&Ls and Balance Sheets to understand the landscape
2. Focus especially on areas where your proposed solutions will help
3. Get prospect's view of trends and future prospects with 'business as usual'
4. Using the metrics baseline you gathered, estimate the gaps – how much improvement is needed in revenue or cost drivers
5. Use the 'Gap' tool on the available CD to suggest improvement targets

The term 'gap' here refers to the amount of underperformance your prospect is experiencing on any metric that matters.

How much improvement is needed? How effectively does your solution address that need? And does your prospect recognize and care about that need?

These are obvious critical early questions in the sales process, and suggest the hard work required to tailor your solution for maximum impact and to earn trusted advisor status.

To measure the gaps, and speak authoritatively to their significance, you will need to review the financials in the prospect's Annual Report or SEC 10K to understand the landscape, starting with your prospect's performance in his or her industry. If your prospect is a private company that doesn't share financial information, gather as much as possible recognizing that it will require more creativity to provide a compelling financial picture. (If you are not fluent in finance, you can review the Chapters in Part 2 that address financial concepts.)

You will also need to understand the drivers of finance, such as the headcount and annual cost per head in the departments that your solution will improve. The worksheet on the facing page demonstrates several approaches for estimating the gaps and potential impacts. (This worksheet is on the available CD supplement.)

Metric: Reduced Staff - any type of production

Current output per person per hour	17.35	Measure this
Desired	25	Get this aspiration from the prospect
Gap	7.65	Calculated
Pre Cent Improvement	44%	Calculated
Number of People	52	Get this from Accounting
Cost per Person-Hour	15.00	Get this from Accounting
Value per Shift	343.92	Calculated
Shifts	3	Get this from Accounting
Value per Day	1,031.76	Calculated
Potential Annual Value	376,592	Calculated (365 days in this example)
Your Solution's Impact %	15%	
Potential Annual Value	56,489	Calculated - and you must demonstrate why this is true

Metric: Staff Reduction - top down estimate

Persons Impacted	25	Get this from Accounting
Cost per Person	48,000	Get this from Accounting
Productivity Improvement %	20%	
Potential Annual Value	240,000	Calculated - and you must demonstrate why this is true

Metric: Increased Production (any type - part, product, operation, or transaction)

Current output per person per hour	17.35	Measure this
Desired	25	Get this aspiration from the prospect
Gap	7.65	Calculated
Value per Unit	220.00	Get this from Accounting
Value per Shift	1,683.00	Calculated
Shifts	3	Get this from Accounting
Value per Day	5,049.00	Calculated
Potential Annual Value	1,842,885	Calculated
Your Solution's Impact %	30%	
Potential Annual Value	552,866	Calculated - and you must demonstrate why this is true

Define the Solution and Deployment Plan

To close a sale, your solution will have to be compelling in its scope and logic, without any significant errors. Your prospect will be relentless in asking:

o Exactly WHAT are you going to deliver and do?
o Exactly HOW does this affect the gaps we have agreed?
o Exactly WHEN will we see measurable results?
o Exactly WHEN will the financial results appear?

Sales Tip

To close a sale, the solution delivery plan must be tightly aligned with the promised financial and non-financial benefits.

The business case must be closely linked to the solution plan and as intuitive as possible, with accurate math and a clear schedule. For example, if equipment is to be installed, provide a realistic estimate of how long it will take to place it in line, train users, troubleshoot/debug and adjust, and ramp up to full speed, and align the timing of the investments required with the financial return. Nothing will kill a sale faster – or deader – than tripping seriously in linking the solution to the expected financial results.

To avoid a misfire, use graphics to help keep you and your prospect on the same page. With the following illustrations, describing the investment and benefits timing and amount will be relatively straightforward.

Here is an example of a high level view of a large Lean/Six Sigma project:

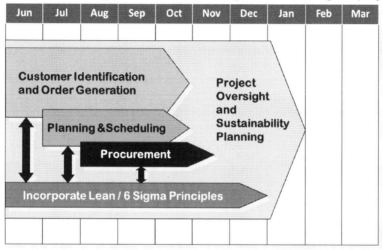

And here is an example of a Program Evaluation and Review Technique (PERT) chart outlining the construction of a house:

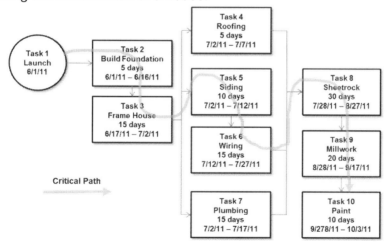

Employy Opportunity Charts

Sales Tip

You can't start improving anything until people agree It is broken, fixable, and worth it.

Step-by-Step

1. Use a format such as the example shown on the facing page or that on the available CD (in the 'Opportunity ID' file)
2. Continuously apply financial analysis to each chart, asking
   a. Accurate data?
   b. Sound logic?
   c. Solid documentation?
3. Link the business case directly to the charts to ensure understanding and agreement

As the sales team investigates an opportunity, it is important to organize information to keep solution plans aligned with expected results. This is supported by 'Opportunity Charts' such as that illustrated below. These are integral to an iterative series of presentations early in the sales process, in which decision makers vet the team's observations and conclusions.

Opportunity charts must be supported by adequately thorough and unimpeachably accurate data, sound logic linking suggested actions with the financial estimates created, and clear documentation of these. There will be no sale until the decision makers are agreed that the solution logic is compelling.

Improvement Opportunity:

Project _____
Process Owner _____
Team Member _____

Current State	**Action Plan**	**Future State**
Problem Statement	**Methodology**	**Description**
What is the problem? What are the symptoms? What are the probable root causes?	What can be done to improve the situation?	What will be different? How will it be better? (Financial and non-financial)
Baseline Metrics	**Investments and Risks**	**Improvement**
What resources are being expended? •Material costs •Machine time •People time •Inventory •Other	What resources are required? •Improvement team •Machinery & equipment additions •Information technology additions •New operating costs – people, machines, etc. When will the investments be made?	What resources will be saved? •Material costs •Machine time •People time •Inventory •Other When will these savings show up? How long will they last?

Calculate the Financial Benefits

The first question to ask of any project is, "what will the benefits be?" Benefits can fall into many categories, such as increased customer or employee satisfaction, productivity gains, and financial performance improvement. In this book we are primarily focused on the financial impacts, and on how your offering promises to return more than it costs.

Promises are easy to make, and unsupported enthusiasm common among people with pet projects. Every benefit estimated needs to be carefully vetted (but not to the point of analysis paralysis). Financial benefits may include:

- o New or enhanced revenue
- o Lower cost of goods (labor, material, or factory efficiency improvements)
- o Lower corporate overhead
- o Better asset utilization (for example, improved inventory turns) providing one-time balance sheet improvements.

Of course, you will need to address the non-financial benefits as well. For example, your prospects may care about:

- o Less hassle and confusion in their business processes
- o Expanded collaboration among their internal and external business partners
- o Quicker time-to-market
- o Higher quality products and services
- o Better social image or government relationships…

The list goes on, so develop the habit of listening carefully for what your prospects care about.

.

Calculate ALL the Costs

In an effort to ensure complete buy-in to your ROI estimates, provide as accurate and complete an analysis of costs as you do of benefits. This honest approach is critical to your credibility as a trusted advisor.

Costs are often more reliably estimated and more controllable than expected benefits, but still leave plenty of room for judgment. Your prospects may be too optimistic about what it will take – many people tend to underestimate the effort required to achieve sizable results. Be sure to set expectations so that you can under-promise and over-deliver.

Sales Tip

The lower and more controllable the costs, the more probable the sale.

With business products, services, and solutions, costs might include such elements as:

- The time of people whose work will need to be done by others during the installation or implementation of your solution
- Costs of internal and external experts / consultants
- Any equipment required to install or use the solution

You should also consider 'Opportunity Cost' – the cost of NOT gaining an alternative financial benefit of an investment. For example, if an owned asset or resource is applied to project A, it will not be available for an alternative project B. The opportunity cost associated with project A is the value of the asset or resource if it were applied to project B. Opportunity costs should be thought of as investments.

It is also important to recognize 'sunk' costs – costs already incurred (paid or obligated), and therefore not relevant to an investment decision.

Calculate the TOTAL Return on Investment

This illustration shows a summary chart and information highlights for a typical Business Case analysis. The content can vary, but a complete analysis should include such ROI indicators as:

o   Cash Flow Payback Curve showing high, expected, and low cases for two years by month
o   Five year summary of expected case benefits, investments and net impact
o   Internal Rate of Return (IRR) and Net Present Value (NPV)

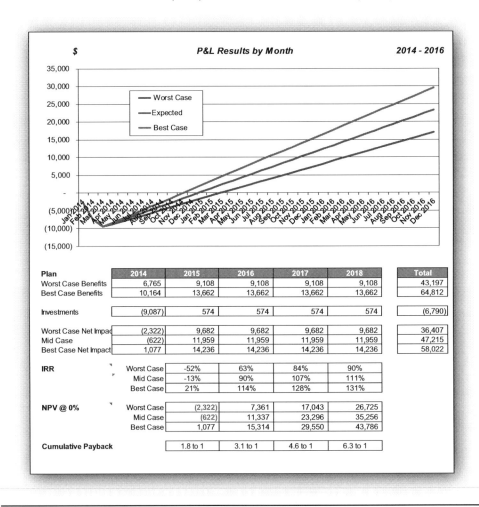

Plan	2014	2015	2016	2017	2018		Total
Worst Case Benefits	6,765	9,108	9,108	9,108	9,108		43,197
Best Case Benefits	10,164	13,662	13,662	13,662	13,662		64,812
Investments	(9,087)	574	574	574	574		(6,790)
Worst Case Net Impac	(2,322)	9,682	9,682	9,682	9,682		36,407
Mid Case	(622)	11,959	11,959	11,959	11,959		47,215
Best Case Net Impact	1,077	14,236	14,236	14,236	14,236		58,022

IRR						
	Worst Case	-52%	63%	84%	90%	
	Mid Case	-13%	90%	107%	111%	
	Best Case	21%	114%	128%	131%	

NPV @ 0%						
	Worst Case	(2,322)	7,361	17,043	26,725	
	Mid Case	(622)	11,337	23,296	35,256	
	Best Case	1,077	15,314	29,550	43,786	

Cumulative Payback		1.8 to 1	3.1 to 1	4.6 to 1	6.3 to 1	

The sales team creates the business case for only one purpose, to show the value and ROI that make your solution compelling.

During the ROI discussions with your prospect, it may prove useful to use a flexible ROI calculating tool in order to answer sales team and buyer 'what if?' questions quickly and accurately. For this reason, the available CD business case tool has presentation page controls for several commonly switched variables:

o   A check box makes it easy to see the difference between P&L and Cash Flow effects.
o   Slide bars allow easy evaluation of different rates for carrying costs (financial cost of owning and caring for assets such as equipment, hardware, software, and inventory), tax rates, and discount (investment hurdle).
o   A final slide bar sets the first year, for user-friendly set up.

Step-by-Step

Use the Business Case worksheet on the available CD to develop a robust and credible financial case for your buyer. The Excel workbook calculator guides you to enter your estimates of the benefits and investments using simple formats, and the entries will be used to calculate the financial impact for up to five years by month. The results are then summarized for executive presentation, showing a payback curve, Net Present Value, and Internal Rate of Return.

The calculator contains pre-loaded data as an example, which you will want to delete before loading your data.

Identify Any and All Risks

If there were no risks in business, there would be no rationale for business profits. Laborers would earn wages and materials would change hands at exactly their value. But in fact everything about business entails risk, including your solution. For examples:

- o   Will the INVESTMENT be as advertised?
- o   Will the SCHEDULE be as expected?
- o   Will it work EXACTLY as advertised?
- o   Will the BENEFITS be as expected?

Sensitivity tests help analysts visualize what might happen if an investment under or over performs, and to develop contingency plans. Typical sensitivity analysis considers a worst case scenario, to ensure business viability is not threatened, and a best case scenario, to set stretch goals for the team that will deliver the results.

There are often specific and predictable possibilities to be considered, calling for scenario planning to estimate their impact on your solution. For example, if you are selling high-efficiency turbine engines and the price of fuel drops significantly, so will your buyer's return on the investment (and of course the returns would be increased if fuel prices rose).

Think out of the box about how your solution can fall short of expectations, and how you can prevent buyer's remorse. Murphy's Law is alive and well!

.

Present a Financial and non-Financial Narrative

While much of a business case addresses the ever-important financial side of a purchase decision, always remember that purchase decisions are as complex as the people making them. In the Part 2 chapter 'Consider Your Customer's Feelings' you will find references to the political and emotional aspects of decisions and to an organization's readiness for change (and your solution is a change).

Your narrative – the structure and content of your sales presentation – will take on a life of its own in your buyer's organization, so it must clearly explain:

> ## Sales Tip
>
> The deal win strategy is not just about affordable cost, but a financial business case showing substantial ROI while meeting the prospective customer's business needs (challenges and desires). Together, this compelling approach gets senior management attention and dramatically improves the probability of closing a sale.

- o How your solution will help the buyer's company financially
- o How your solution will make life easier for the buyers and their organizations
- o How your solution will enhance your buyers' careers / personal wins
- o How your solution will improve business operations in line with the buyer's vision, with minimal organizational disruption

Step 5:
In a confirmation meeting with the EB in attendance, demonstrate the product, verify how the ROI will be achieved, and outline the proposal. Activities include:

- o Confirm that the EB will provide post presentation / demonstration review time
- o Open with the value proposition presentation outlining the prioritized needs and monetized value
- o Demonstrate the product laced with anecdotes directly from survey information from the prospective customer organization

- o Throughout the course of the demonstration get confirming buy-in from the group, showing they are engaged and envision this as their solution. NOTE: Resistance must be dealt with accurately and respectfully. STOP the demonstration and RESCHEDULE if key decision makers are not in agreement with the solution.
- o At the conclusion meet with the EB and confirm his / her pleasure with the buy-in of his / her team and to plan next steps. If ready, provide a first draft of the proposed contract.
  - If not at this post demo meeting, set up a meeting closely following this one to review contracts and verify approval steps necessary for final sign-off (approvals, signatures, legal reviews, procurement, and timetable).

In the next chapter we will put this all together and prepare to close the sale.

Close the Sale

Get to 'Yes,' Map the Gates, and Drive the Timelines

Sales Tip

Closing a sale is more than gaining commitment. For many organizations, before a PO is initiated and a contract is signed, there can be a multi-step process comprised of business case reviews and multiple sign-offs. Know the process and timing, so you can be proactive in assisting with gates that may get closed on the deal. This will increase your ability to get the contract signed and will improve your forecast accuracy.

In a complex sale, there remains much to be done between the successful product demonstration and the closing. These pre-closing activities require the same attention to detail that got the buyer ready to select and move forward with your solution / proposal. During these final two steps the objectives are to continue to reinforce the value and ROI with the EB and to facilitate the approval process, managing any gates that could affect final contract approval.

Step 6:

Plan post-demonstration meetings and have documents ready in draft form. Activities include:

- o Verify the Prospective customer's intent to move forward and handle any objections
- o Review each step of the approval process leading to a signed contract. Most of these will already be known, but get deep into the process so you know the who and when of each of the approval gates, legal review steps, and procurement steps

- o Schedule short interval follow-ups to keep the process moving, and to know where it stands at all times. Your Champion and EB have other job priorities that will hold their attention, so you need to monitor it closely – this is YOUR priority.
- o Reinforce the ROI and value proposition with your Champion and EB, so they

become fluent with it and are able to overcome any internal questions that arise. Help them see that every day, week or month delay in getting this product/solution contract approved and deployed is delaying the realization of operating improvements, cost savings, and ROI that comes with the purchase.

Sales Tip

Typically the larger the prospective client, the longer the approval process takes due to the breadth of the organization and approval levels involved.

Step 7:
Negotiate the final contract and close. Activities include:

- Maintain constant contact with the Champion and the EB as they run interference with the internal approval process
- Keep them fluent with the ROI, value propositions and business benefits so they can use that for their own internal business case. You want them to be able to take on your role internally and they should be fully bought into doing that at this point.
- Identify and manage any risks to overcome (such as legal Terms and Conditions) proactively
- Obtain the signed contract.
- Immediately plan, or begin, the post-contract deployment process.

Closing Techniques

It all starts with 'earning the right' to ask for the business. You have done considerable work to get to steps 6 and 7 of the ROI Driven Sales Process, where you will get to yes, map the gates, and drive the timelines. To make the sale, you have:

- Qualified your prospective customers Interest and Intent
- Built further interest in your solution – at high and wide levels of the buyers organization
- Established the value of your solution in a collaborative setting with your prospect
- Created and tested Value Propositions, ROI's and a Business Case showing a dramatic upside
- Presented the winning business case
- Achieved Trusted Advisor status with your prospect by
  - Offering highly credible new ideas and
  - Proving you are focused on helping the prospective customer, not on simply making a sale
- Continued to validate the interest and intent along the sales cycle timeline
- Achieved buy-in from multiple levels including the Economic Buyer and other key influencers.

If you have executed the above steps effectively and have been qualifying as you go (testing the level of interest and intent and validating budget and timing), then the prospect will certainly expect you to ask for the order.

So…. it should be as easy as saying "let's get started!"

But 7 out of 10 times it isn't that easy, because as much as you try to ensure there are no surprises…

- There may still be others who need to sign off
- Business issues may have arisen (such as poor quarterly performance, announcement of a reduction in force (RIF), or the like)

- o The prospective buyer now back-tracks as to their signatory power or budgetary control
- o Unexpected changes of key personnel

Expect the unexpected, but minimize the impact by diligently, effectively executing all the necessary steps throughout the sales cycle.

As with any part of the sales cycle, you need to prepare for whatever situation arises as the end approaches. Your progress through the above seven steps will determine when and who you will work with at the end to ensure you keep the selling process moving towards closure. But of course you won't wait until Step 6 & 7 to deal with the unexpected. At regular interval trial closes and as a natural part of your communications, you will have used questioning techniques such as these:

Assumptive Question / Close / Trial-Close:

Tactic	Ask the client a question for which their answer can imply that they will make a purchase.
Example	"So if the product could do X you'd be ready to move ahead?"
Remark (Caution)	If you have already established and have buy-in for this capability, it may seem too assuming for some prospects.

Concession Question / Close / Trial-Close:

Tactic	You offer the client a concession in order to close the deal.
Example	"If I can reduce your cost by 10% can we move ahead?"
Remark	This is all about positioning and in today's climate, it is an effective technique that can help you gain quick favor with new prospective clients. Every buyer wants to feel they are getting a deal. Remember you have established value and have shown a favorable ROI so any price reduction should be kept to a minimum or you are eroding the value you established.

Opportunity-Cost Question / Close / Trial-Close:

Tactic	Whether it is money, productivity or time, there is always a cost associated with not buying. Show them what it is and why your solution is the answer.
Example	"Similar Customers using this solution have seen a 55% increase in productivity and cost savings of 25% over the first 3

	years."
Remark	This is a great technique especially for high price solutions because the potential gains or long term savings can then be weighed against the initial price. Moreover, it is a great opportunity to draw attention to others in the same industry that may also be using your solution.

Summary Question / Close / Trial-Close:

Tactic	Summarize everything that has been discussed, list off all deliverables and make a comment to close.
Example	"So we have been through the product, answered all of your questions and are set to deliver ten seats of our enterprise package. Let's finalize the paperwork and establish the deployment timeframe."
Remark	This is a favorite because it allows everyone to confirm that you are on the same page. It eliminates any surprises upon delivery and it drastically helps reduce the chances of buyer's remorse.

Direct Question / Close / Trial-close:

Tactic	Have the confidence to ask if the deal is closing by asking an obvious question that is direct and to the point.
Example	"We have worked together to be in the position to have a quantifiable solution, it sounds like I've answered all of your questions, is it safe to assume we are ready to move forward?"
Remark (Caution)	Similar to the Assumptive question, you need to have a good read on your prospect in order to use this technique. This approach is good, because it gives the prospect an out. It demonstrates your confidence and your understanding of their challenges and desires and without the pressure of the first option.

Remember that questions such as these and trial-closes throughout the sales cycle are a natural way to ensure all parties know where everyone collectively stands at all times, and that the interest and intent remain intact.

Follow Up

So the sale is made – great! But your job isn't done quite yet. With complex sales, tossing a contract over the wall to the delivery team is worse even than catching an undeveloped lead from the marketing team, because your company's reputation depends on the consistent quality of EVERY customer experience. You worked too hard to become a trusted advisor to erode the good will with delivery missteps.

Sales Tip

There is nothing as good for your marketing and sales efforts as a satisfied customer – and nothing worse than an angry one.

Most vendors have a formal internal handoff process to ensure what has been sold is clearly understood by the delivery organization. If yours does not, it is well worth considering how you will ensure that what you have promised will be delivered.

PART 2: SPEAK YOUR PROSPECTIVE CUSTOMER'S LANGUAGE

Your customers are kept up at night by increasing pressure to cut costs and improve efficiencies leading to comprehensive business and product improvements and financial results. Your product, service, or solution might be just what they need, and you will be their trusted, empathic, creative advisor when you are fluent in the issues that weigh heaviest on their minds.

- o Every executive should have a vision of his or her company's business model (how it makes money), its systems for management (how it steers itself), and its business processes (how it executes its mission). Chapter 8 provides cutting edge insights into how virtually every operation works. How will your offerings fit into this vision?

- o Companies use metrics and key performance Indicators to track and control the performance of practically everything they do. Many are informal and only a few, in larger enterprises, are integrated into an effective executive dashboard. Chapter 9 provides the principles behind excellent systems of metrics. We touched on this briefly in Chapter 5 – you need metrics to understand the impact of your solution on your customer's business. Read Chapter 9 and take on added authority.

- o Do you know much about Lean / Six Sigma tools and techniques? Every sophisticated organization does. Chapter 10 provides a primer so you won't be left on the periphery of an important conversation involving your offering.

- o Every business person needs to be financially literate. Higher level executives are, with very few exceptions. If you want to talk with them, read Chapter 11. If you want to get them excited, read Chapter 12.

- o The world runs on sophisticated IT systems and whatever you're selling will very probably be controlled by or incorporated into them. Chapter 13 provides a basic overview.

- o Finally, <u>Chapter 14</u> talks about how people deal with change – and every sale is a change. No one cares how much you know until they know how much you care. If you only read one chapter this should be it!

Understand Your Prospective Customer's Operating Vision

A Tool for Rapid Insight into Any Business

Elevator Pitch

"An operating vision – of how a company makes money, manages itself, and executes its processes – shared by most or all employees greatly facilitates communication and cooperation for success."

Your sales role as a trusted advisor requires that you understand many aspects of your prospective customer's business. As a guide for rapidly gaining this understanding, we have developed the 'Vision Tool,' a compilation of multiple tools and techniques designed to analyze virtually any business at a high level. It is not about a catch-phrase to focus employees, but rather about a view of how the business should function.

The Vision Tool encompasses three elements describing how well the business works, as illustrated here:

1. Business Model: Is the company positioning itself for maximum success in its industry?
2. Systems for Management: Are executive and management structure and practices optimal for success?
3. Operating Processes: Are the work processes optimal for delivering value and operating effectively and efficiently?

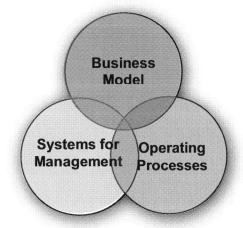

An organization's specific vision for the future can be developed from the aspirations of its people, recognizing the cultural factors that will influence timing and sequencing. A road map to achieve the vision can be based on the gaps and their significance, and sequencing must address root causes (foundational elements) as well as cultural readiness for change. A business case will be needed to consider the estimated costs and benefits of the road map. All of these tools and techniques are described in this book.

Business Effectiveness Attributes

Every organization has a 'business model,' describing why it exists and how it serves its customers. For commercial enterprises, this describes how it makes money. For government and non-profit organizations it describes how funds are secured and used for its constituents. Secondly, it needs sound management in an organized structure. Thirdly, it requires processes that effectively and efficiently execute its business model. For each of these aspects of business, key attributes have been defined. These key attributes vary by business, but the set in this chapter is generally useful as a starting point for analyzing commercial enterprises.

For each attribute, a set of five maturity descriptors will help to identify weaknesses and determine where your prospect needs to focus improvement efforts. Each attribute can be evaluated in terms of how well or poorly it is executed. Descriptors on the maturity grids suggest a progressively better executed (more mature) operation (1 is low, 5 is high). Using these attributes, you can identify the prospect's challenges and aspirations and provide ideas for improvement.

Insiders – the economic buyer and the decision influencers – will generally have

---

Step-by-Step

Gather information on how well-developed and effective the vision is:

1. Ask the key movers in the company, generally executives plus highly-regarded managers and thought leaders
2. Collect the responses and create a chart to compare 'As Is' view and an aspirational 'To Be' view
3. Analyze the gaps. Are they important?
4. Apply your solution to the gaps. Does it help close them?
5. Iteratively develop a path forward with the executives, addressing foundational weaknesses as well as high-impact fixes

strong and often accurate opinions, so discussing the concepts in these maturity grids with them will provide you with material to inspire new thinking and new approaches, and ultimately to offering your product or solution.

In reviewing a company's Business Model, look for the clarity and intuitive nature of the model; broad understanding and alignment with cultural norms; and resources allocated to each attribute.

Systems for Management should show strong leadership presence; logic and clarity of organization structure, policies, practices, and IT systems; and an educated and resourceful workforce.

Operating Processes in the factory or the office should be optimized with clear, logical flow, roles and responsibilities, minimum errors, wheel-spinning and rework; minimum wasted motion and unnecessary activity; reasonable flow speed; care appropriate to the value passing through critical processes; and minimum wait time. These should result in high internal and external customer satisfaction.

Maturity Grids

Maturity grids can help you gain an understanding and organize ideas about a prospective organization's effectiveness, and communicate those ideas. Following are maturity grids for each of the three Vision Tool elements.

Business Model Maturity Grid

		1 - Weak	2	3	4	5 - Strong
1	**Business Intelligence** - competitive analysis and Benchmarking to ensure optimum capabilities	Little concept of competing companies or technologies. No benchmarks for any aspect of the business.	Occasional competitive analysis and benchmarking.	Benchmarks are commonly used to ensure practices are competitive.	Ongoing competitive analysis and benchmarking provide assurance that the organization is effective and efficient.	All competitive actions and capabilities are analyzed and incorporated in strategic plans.
2	**Voice of the Customer** - customer feedback and market analysis to ensure products and services are well targeted	Little understanding of what customers / potential customers want or what they need.	Customer satisfaction surveys are used occasionally to deal with suspected problems.	Customer feedback informs all major product and market actions.	Customer surveys include rewards to customers for providing product improvement insights.	Formal programs ensure that customer attitudes, wants and needs are fully understood and used in product / market plans.
3	**Strategic Direction** - vision, and the strategies to achieve it	No clearly articulated vision of the future or strategy to ensure success.	Executives have a shared vision and a published strategy, but not widely shared.	The vision and strategy are clearly articulated to the organization.	Vision and strategy are developed with input from leaders throughout the organization.	Strategic direction is set using processes that ensure the best intelligence and ideas of the whole organization are incorporated.
4	**Financial Management**- accounting, control, cash planning, and profitability analysis	Bookkeeping, basic financial statements, limited financial metric tracking.	Strong accounting and control disciplines ensure accurate and timely information.	Budgets, variance reports and key ratios ensure spending is controlled and sensible.	A clear and well-designed financial analysis package provides the right metrics at the right time to each decision maker.	Focus is on shareholder value through ongoing analysis of operations, investments, and capital sourcing.

Business Model (cont'd)

		1 - Weak	2	3	4	5 - Strong
5	**Capital Investments** - capital productivity analysis and ROI analysis	Limited capital planning, without substantial business cases for CAPEX.	Business cases are used for spending decisions, each case treated as unique, and analysis approaches often reinvented.	Major investments are evaluated using sophisticated business cases.	Standardized business cases provide a level playing field for all capital investment decisions.	Capital investments are continuously analyzed to ensure optimum configuration for return on investment.

Systems for Management Maturity Grid

		1 - Weak	2	3	4	5 - Strong
6	**Organization Structure-** spans of control, functional skills and process alignment	Legacy organization structure may or may not meet any particular functional or operating requirements as the business evolves.	Organizational structure is redefined to resolve specific problems, building on the strengths of specific individuals.	Organizational structure is based on norms (such as spans of control) for the type of business, and benchmarks/consultants help when changes are needed.	The organization is matrixed, with strong leadership of functions and of processes.	Processes are continuously improved and organization structure is continuously aligned for functional excellence and process efficiency.
7	**Decision Making Processes -** authority structure, formats, and practices	Executive and management decisions by gut feel. Weak controls and uncoordinated criteria.	Sound controls are in place, with clear approval authorities and commonly understood (but informal) criteria in place.	Decisions are made at appropriate levels based on appropriate data, but often take excessive time.	Executive focus has improved the decision process. Most decisions are timely and appropriate based on relevant data.	Optimum decisions are made quickly following clear processes with clear criteria.
8	**Communications & Alignment -** audiences, media, and messages	Most operating information is promulgated ad hoc following personal relationships.	Formal communications are sent regularly but without targeting, resulting in information overload.	Key information is well-managed, but important information is sometimes missed.	Most information is available when and where needed, through multiple formal and informal methods.	Communications are well-managed to ensure operations are coordinated and the organization is aligned.
9	**Human Relations Policy & Practice -** rewards and recognition	Human resource management is not seen as strategically important.	Key HR activities such as hiring and firing are highly valued and effectively managed. The policy manual is current and accessible.	HR effectively manages employee needs and plays a key role in rewards and recognition.	HR leads training efforts to ensure all critical skills are available at all times.	HR is organizationally positioned as a critical part of the business.

Systems for Management (Cont'd)

		1 - Weak	2	3	4	5 - Strong
10	**Executive Sponsorship** - visibility and focus	Executives are rarely visible to the workforce.	Executives kick things off but are generally difficult to involve in day to day action.	Executives practice 'management by walking around,' and are aware of all key activities in their areas of responsibility.	Executives sponsor key activities and participate as needed to make things work.	Executives are clearly visible sponsoring every critical activity of the organization, especially business changes, and participate in cross-functional steering teams.
11	**Scheduling & Priority Setting** - schedule management, emergency management	Firefighting is common, and work schedules are routinely interrupted.	Schedules are well-managed, but can be badly disrupted by emergency work.	The scheduling process anticipates emergency work, but excessive overtime still occurs routinely.	Scheduling is a focus area, and a rapid decision process supports schedule interruption decisions.	Priorities are so well managed that schedules are seldom interrupted and deadlines are routinely met without stress.
12	**Hiring, Retention, & Succession Planning** - critical skills coverage and continuity	Retirements and unplanned absences can bring the operation to its knees.	Desk procedures and common knowledge repositories ensure retirements and unplanned absences do not impact critical tasks.	Training programs are designed to build skills progressively, with a pipeline of candidates for every planned vacancy.	Building and maintaining critical skills is seen as a strategic activity, and executives participate as needed to ensure uninterrupted capability.	Retirements and unplanned absences have little effect on the business, and critical skills will remain secure.
13	**Education, Training & Skill Flexibility** - training program, task competence, work interruption	Few employees are fully trained for their work and almost none are cross-trained.	Functional departments have cross-training programs to ensure department work is never stopped by an absence.	Job rotation creates informal workforce flexibility, with many people capable of filling in for multiple tasks across functional lines.	The organization focuses on cross-training, and employees are rewarded for broad skills serving multiple process tasks. Skills are formally tracked to anticipate skill needs.	All employees are fully trained for their work and multiple resources are skilled for every significant task in every key process.

Operating Processes Maturity Grid

		1 - Weak	2	3	4	5 - Strong
14	**Marketing & Sales** - Income generation and sales funnel management	There is no sales funnel tracking, and future sales are highly uncertain.	The sales funnel is defined and unambiguous roles are established for every step.	Quotas are set and followed up to ensure prospects move through the sales funnel.	Realistic quotas are set for every step of the sales funnel, and regular meetings highlight issues early and effectively.	The sales funnel is managed to ensure optimum profitability and growth.
15	**Work Practices** - Standard work and team daily practices	There is no 'standard' work, and no routine method to coordinate work across departments.	Every desk has standard procedures, and all normal tasks are well documented.	Processes are documented and tasks within the processes well defined.	Processes are streamlined and tasks are distributed effectively.	Standard work and 'shift huddles' ensure all work is effectively focused and efficiently performed day to day and for special projects.
16	**Supply Chain**- supplier programs, material movement, and transportation management	Suppliers are not managed formally, even for critical parts. Transportation is treated as a commodity.	The supply chain is mapped and roles are understood.	Suppliers are well-managed, with preferred status and blanket orders routinely applied.	All suppliers, internal and external, are well aware of expectations at all times.	Critical suppliers and transporters are trusted partners, and everything flows smoothly.
17	**Supporting Technologie s** - computer systems and information management	Information systems are an uncoordinated kludge, and critical information is routinely unavailable.	Information systems are integrated and information is readily available.	Information is well organized and easy to access.	Information is organized and structured for hierarchical analysis.	Information is always available when and where needed in an optimum form for immediate use. Critical information is proactively delivered to decision makers.

Operating Processes (Cont'd)

		1 - Weak	2	3	4	5 - Strong
18	**Process Management** - process definitions, flow charts, and process ownership	Processes do not have clear definitions, flow charts, or owners.	Processes are defined and some critical ones are mapped.	Processes are routinely analyzed in order to resolve flow issues.	Most processes are well defined and mapped. Critical processes have owners.	Processes are well defined, mapped, and streamlined, and there are clear owners.
19	**Roles & Responsibilities** - accountability, responsibility, consulting and informing	There is commonly confusion about accountability or responsibility for any task, and who to consult or inform.	Tasks have assigned owners.	Task owners have established and generally understood methods for coordinating their work.	Critical task owners have published RACI (responsible, accountable, consult, inform) lists.	Everyone always knows what they are expected to do, and who to coordinate with for every task.
20	**Teamwork & Integration** - daily work and continuous improvement	'Every man for himself.'	Critical tasks are handled by teams, and teams are rewarded for effective handling of critical processes.	Business improvement is typically handled by cross-functional teams.	Every department sees itself as a team, and every process is seen as a team activity.	Daily work and business improvements are routinely accomplished by cross-functional teams with all the right skills.

Understand the Metrics Your Prospects Use

What Metrics are All About

Metrics provide the information needed to achieve and maintain effectiveness, indicating what executives, owners, and managers care about. When they are aligned with the business vision they help ensure that customers get what they need when they want it, that the company makes money, that employees are motivated and loyal, and that production of goods or services remains effective and efficient.

> ### Elevator Pitch
>
> "What you measure determines what you will achieve."

The most important metrics, referred to as Key Performance Indicators (KPIs), are often compiled regularly for the executive team onto a 'dashboard.' This sharp focus on the right business drivers helps your prospects steer their organization through today's often complex and confusing business environment. Understanding those KPIs gives you an opportunity to offer ideas as a trusted advisor, enjoying a distinct advantage over any competitor who doesn't.

In too many cases metrics simply evolve based on one requirement after another. The misaligned metrics then help drive sub-optimization, unhealthy competition for resources, political maneuvering, duplication of effort, and a variety of other wasteful conditions that rob managers of sleep and shareholders of profits.

This chapter is a quick primer and a reference for creating a highly effective, balanced set of metrics in any organization, containing concepts and examples indicative of the thought process behind an effective metric system. There is a wealth of published information about balanced score cards (e.g., from Kaplan and Norton) and lean accounting (e.g., from Maskell and others) to supplement the topics covered.

Strategic Metrics

Step-by-Step

In creating a measurement system, consider:

o   What are the most important measures, meaning those that reflect the overall success of the business? These should include customer satisfiers, efficiency indicators, and employee satisfiers to ensure an organization's long-term effectiveness.
o   What business functions or departments impact these measures?
o   Can the metrics be combined mathematically (as in the graphic on the next page) or will they need to be combined into a weighted index?

Integrating operational metrics into a broad family of business metrics can help in decision-making throughout a company. Organizations typically develop measurement systems piecemeal, to resolve problems as they occur. The problem with this approach is that it fosters sub-optimization and conflict among managers attempting to drive their piece of the business without comprehending the impact on other areas. For example, the financial team may want to cut inventory while the marketing team attempts to build it.

An interesting visual approach to grasp the impact is to place many of an organization's performance charts onto a single chart. Typically this will result in a confusing array with too many metrics, and with few measurement results tracking well with other measurement results.

When selling, consider who, at what level, your product or solution benefits. By addressing the KPIs at multiple levels, you greatly increase the likelihood that insider buzz in the prospect's organization will be supporting your sales efforts.

An effective system of key metrics will provide a view that makes sense top to bottom, side to side in an organization. The most important indicators will be clearly visible at the top of the organization, as an index or a combined value, and it will be easy to investigate successive lower levels to identify the sources of problems.

Efficiency Index

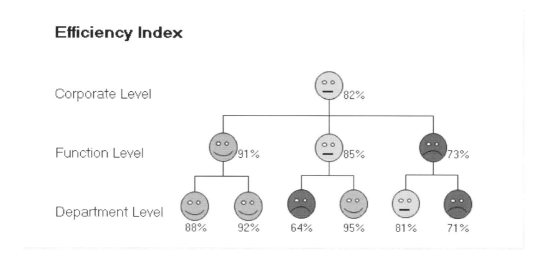

Hierarchy of Metrics

An effective system of metrics has several characteristics:

- It fosters a balanced view, preventing sub-optimization among departments and helping to resolve conflicts between functions or departments.
- It recognizes the role of processes in accomplishing work, and fosters immediate resolution of process issues by operators in the area affected.
- It is hierarchical. Indicators at the highest level can be peeled back to the lowest level with no loss of directional integrity.
- It is minimalist. There are no unnecessary metrics to generate information overload. Metrics are for communication and decision-making - only.
- The mathematics are simple. Wherever possible, it is better to simply add department results than to create complex algorithms that confuse managers and executives.
- It is as visible side-to-side and top-to-bottom as is prudent. The more people can know about the metric structure and actual performance, the better they will understand what drives the business and the better their decisions will be.

The structure suggested on the next page is merely a starting point, but includes some of the most common elements needed to support decision-making.

Sample Hierarchy of Metrics

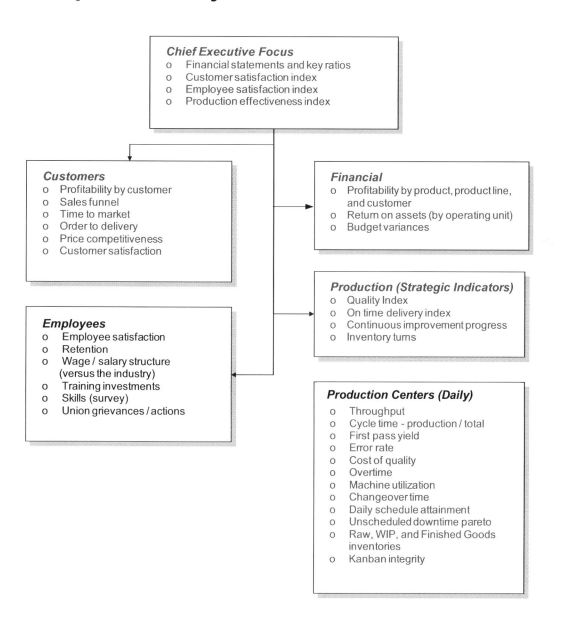

Chief Executive Focus
- o Financial statements and key ratios
- o Customer satisfaction index
- o Employee satisfaction index
- o Production effectiveness index

Customers
- o Profitability by customer
- o Sales funnel
- o Time to market
- o Order to delivery
- o Price competitiveness
- o Customer satisfaction

Financial
- o Profitability by product, product line, and customer
- o Return on assets (by operating unit)
- o Budget variances

Production (Strategic Indicators)
- o Quality Index
- o On time delivery index
- o Continuous improvement progress
- o Inventory turns

Employees
- o Employee satisfaction
- o Retention
- o Wage / salary structure (versus the industry)
- o Training investments
- o Skills (survey)
- o Union grievances / actions

Production Centers (Daily)
- o Throughput
- o Cycle time - production / total
- o First pass yield
- o Error rate
- o Cost of quality
- o Overtime
- o Machine utilization
- o Changeover time
- o Daily schedule attainment
- o Unscheduled downtime pareto
- o Raw, WIP, and Finished Goods inventories
- o Kanban integrity

Balanced Scorecard

Elevator Pitch

"The Balanced Scorecard ensures that executives and managers are setting objectives that consider financial, customer employee, operational and community/ ethical requirements."

The concept of the 'Balanced Scorecard' was introduced in 1993 by Harvard Business School professors Robert Kaplan and David Norton. Like the hierarchy of metrics on the prior pages, it is designed to ensure top management focus on the trade-offs required to achieve interrelated strategic objectives and avoid sub-optimization.

Particular focus is on preventing financial measures from overshadowing other important considerations such as investments for the future, customer and employee satisfaction, ethics, community relations, sales performance, market penetration, and the like.

The Balanced Scorecard can be used to establish specific targets and accountabilities. For example:

OBJECTIVES	TARGETS	ACCOUNTABLE
Financial 1. ROIC 2. Profit margin 3. Etc.		
Customers 1. Satisfaction Index 2. Etc.		
Employees 1. Satisfaction Index 2. Etc.		
Processes 1. Quality 2. Efficiency 3. Etc.		
Marketing 1. Forecast accuracy 2. Campaign effectiveness 3. Market penetration		
Sales 1. Pipeline health 2. Performance to quota		
Community 1. Philanthropy 2. Etc.		

> Other columns could address achievement dates, associated projects / teams, and similar information to support achieving key objectives.

Lean versus Traditional Metrics

Elevator Pitch

"Lean Accounting turns the accounting team loose to focus on business improvements that drive profit."

Lean metrics are best viewed in the context of lean accounting. The key insights of lean accounting are illustrated in this chart in terms of significant contrasts with traditional accounting. Note: Lean accounting is most obviously beneficial in volume production environments.

In traditional, full-absorption accounting, a primary task of accounting is to fix specific costs to every produced item. The costs are typically captured and tracked in units of raw, Work-in-Process (WIP), and finished goods inventories, and become Cost of Goods Sold (COGS) on the Profit and Loss Statement (P&L) as each unit is bought by a customer. Numerous transactions are processed daily to ensure that costs of materials and direct labor are assigned correctly and that production overhead costs are allocated as accurately as possible. That can be a lot of accounting.

By contrast, Lean Accounting focuses on all costs of 'value streams' (start-to-finish work activities associated with individual product families). Because inventories are virtually eliminated or held very stable by in-line kanban rules, costs are streamlined and no longer tracked into and out of inventory. Work cells measure actual WIP versus Standard WIP (SWIP) on an ongoing basis, and over and under conditions receive immediate self-correction at the point of creation. SWIP will be adjusted based on overall plant throughput as volumes rise or fall, and Balance Sheet adjustments can generally be made on an infrequent as-needed basis. In general, the more variety of product and process, the more often lines are stopped and started, the more a company can profit from Lean Operations. Simultaneously, the more a company gains by shifting to Lean Operations, the more it will gain from also shifting to Lean Accounting.

This work reduction frees accounting up for the productive work of helping company strategists focus on uses for available capacity (which typically increases dramatically in a lean environment) and helping line operators identify, prioritize, and capitalize on cost opportunities. Lean Accounting is not less accounting, but it provides a lot more bang for the buck.

Lean vs. Traditional Accounting

Traditional	Lean
o Accounting data drives production decisions	o Production decisions are made based on immediate production metrics
o Every machine needs to run as efficiently as possible - usually by running non-stop	o The overall process is run as efficiently as possible. It's okay for a machine to sit idle when not needed
o Errors are found by inspection and may be blamed on operators	o Errors are assumed to spring from interconnected processes and are resolved at their roots
o Value is tracked in inventories as they work through the production steps, driving continuous, complex calculations	o Cost is tracked at the value stream level. Inventory is calculated based on period throughput and adjusted only as throughput changes

Process versus Result Metrics

Metrics fall into two classes: Process (leading indicators) and Results (historical records). Both are critical to business effectiveness and continuous improvement of business operations.

Process metrics are used on the front lines to ensure the overall operation stays in tune. They indicate that immediate action needs to be taken by the operators and supervisors, adjusting equipment, directing resources, or correcting operators or procedures. They also indicate when longer-term fixes are needed, identifying opportunities to be addressed in Kaizen Events, policy or engineering change requests, etc., under the continuous improvement rubric. These metrics are further used as key analytical input in addressing issues.

Process	*Results*
o Predictive, future-oriented o Early warning o Day-to-day o For operating decisions	o Historical o Longer-term view o Periodic (Quarter, Year) o For strategic decisions
Examples o Statistical quality o Daily throughput o First pass yield o On time delivery	*Examples* o Financial Statements o Cost & profit analyses o Customer Sat Survey o Employee Sat Survey

Results metrics are used by executive management to formulate strategies and institute policies and guidelines for operations. Financial information indicates how well investments are performing and informs further investment and financing decisions. Customer satisfaction data helps establish marketing and sales strategies and resource allocations. Employee satisfaction and comparative salary data helps set hiring, training, rewards and recognition, and expansion and reduction plans and policies.

Process metrics, rolled up and accumulated over time, also help executives in establishing policy and strategy, and are especially useful in support of continuous improvement.

Customer Metrics

Philip Crosby defined quality as conformance to requirements, with primary emphasis on customer requirements. This implies that market survival and growth in an increasingly quality-conscious environment are fueled by knowledge of customer needs and wants, and require metrics that ensure alignment. The chart illustrates the kind of metrics that inform product and service decisions.

What customers value	What to measure
Unique designs	Changeover / available operating time at plant
Time to market	Concept to production cycle
Ruggedness, appearance	o First time quality o Life time quality o PPM
Availability	o Order to promise o On time delivery
Price	Index to competition o At the dealer o To the trade
Attention and customer service	Customer satisfaction

Note particularly that customers generally want personalized service, and to be treated as valued, important business partners. Relationship selling has been impacted by the Internet and the expectation of 'getting a deal,' but people still buy, when they can, from people they know and trust. If you want customer loyalty, never lose sight of how customers perceive your relationship with them. Metrics can help.

It is important to recognize, of course, that customer loyalty needs to be traded off with profitability. There are significant differences between being 'customer driven' and 'customer compelled,' and the metrics suggested along with benchmarks (comparisons with the offerings of other companies) can help identify the boundaries in your industry.

Financial Metrics

Financial metrics are fairly standard across industries, but often misused, even in the rigidly controlled environment created by Sarbanes-Oxley. Some of the common misapplications include:

o   CEOs, and headquarters organizations, sometimes review results and dictate cost cuts (often necessary) without considering whether their operating divisions or production facilities have the tools and skills to deliver the cuts without seriously damaging the business.
o   Executive teams are often too focused on the short term.
o   Subsidiary elements are sometimes required to report information at levels so low that headquarters organizations couldn't possibly analyze it properly. Any resulting headquarters micro-management can only confuse and demoralize operators and misapply resources.
o   Weak financial direction can confound decision-making with shifting investment methodologies and criteria.

What stockholders value	What to measure
Return on assets	Profit after tax / assigned assets
Product management	Profitability by product or product line
Utilization of resources	Profit per employee
Investment management	Business cases Results tracking

Financial metrics should be recognized for the trailing indicators they are, valuable for strategic direction setting but less useful for tactical decisions.

Employee Metrics

Employees on the front lines accomplish the vast majority of the work of a company, and are rightly considered the most important resources in enlightened organizations. The overwhelming majority of workers want to create value efficiently to protect their income, their retirement options, and their pride of workmanship. For this reason they are generally delighted at the opportunity to participate in improving product quality and process efficiency, and to provide a fair output for their fair salaries and wages.

What employees value	What to measure
o Fair wages / salaries	o Employee satisfaction
o Interesting work	o Retention
o Advancement opportunity	o Wage / salary structure versus the industry
o Pleasant working conditions	o Training investments
	o Skills (survey)
	o Union grievances / actions

Metrics help an organization know what they must pay to get skilled people and how employees see the environment created. Training programs are created and revised to ensure people are getting what they need, and metrics identify the gaps. Critical skills and succession planning are directly influenced by meaningful skills and retention data, exit interviews, and surveys. In most organizations, executive and managerial effectiveness depends directly on knowing their employees very, very well.

Production Metrics

Production, in manufacturing and non-manufacturing settings, is a minute-by-minute phenomenon, and process metrics can help make near-instantaneous adjustments to prevent any substantial problematic output. When operating teams have immediate awareness of out-of-spec products, they can adjust equipment, focus skills, escalate the problem for higher level review, or stop production as needed to prevent increasingly expensive downstream problems.

Lean operations - relentlessly reducing waste - depend on meaningful, accurate measurement of every critical production parameter. This chart illustrates some useful performance measurement concepts. Your operations may have additional parameters to measure, beyond the effectiveness, efficiency, schedule, and inventory considerations illustrated, but this is a good starting point.

What the Process Needs	What to measure
o Production effectiveness	o Throughput o Cycle time - production / total o First pass yield o Error rate o Cost of quality
o Production efficiency (Minimum wasted time / resources)	o Overtime o Machine utilization o Changeover time
o Schedule integrity	o Daily schedule attainment o Unscheduled downtime pareto
o Minimum inventory	o Raw, WIP, and Finished Goods inventories o Kanban integrity

Metrics Terminology

Metrics typically fall into the categories discussed above, but with many variations of emphasis and terminology. For example, metrics for 'production' or 'customers' in a hospital will use industry-specific terms unfamiliar in a bank or a manufacturing facility. The terminology is important, for rapid and clear communication in a given environment, and professionals must learn the native language of their chosen field thoroughly and quickly to be successful.

Benchmarking

Metrics are a logical starting point for benchmarking and for identifying best practices. The chart illustrates a logical sequence and some key considerations for an organization adopting a benchmarking philosophy.

But however popular, benchmarking is a commonly misunderstood concept. Some executives appear to believe that their organization's efficiency and effectiveness can be controlled by fiat, and that simply informing employees about demonstrated better performance will generate improvements. However, benchmarks and best practices can be misleading, and employees will be demoralized if they see no path to their goals.

o   Business is seldom done the same way by any two companies, however similar to their products and markets. For example, one company may rely on an ERP system for its information backbone, while another may for legitimate reasons handle its transactions more manually, resulting in very different overhead cost structures.

o   Best practices may not be appropriate. 'Good enough' may be good enough. For example, a manufacturing organization typically does not need to process its transactions as fast or efficiently as a financial institution, even though with enough investment it could.

o   Benchmark databases vary in quality, depending on the insights and purposes of the organization that created them and on the survey instruments and populations used to generate them.

Despite these concerns, benchmarks can be useful as all the bars in business are continuously raised. The key is to track the right indicators and to continuously seek ways to lead the pack through continuous improvement.

Considering Benchmarking?

Establishing	Ensure that...

1. Ensure that your metrics are measuring the things that matter to the business
 	
2. Find the organizations that keep databases of measures for the applicable industry
 	
3. Review available benchmarking data bases to ensure:
 	
   o Comparability to your operations
 	
   o Useful focus and trend information
 	
   o Best practice identification
 	
4. Train an internal team to analyze and interpret data and set goals
 	
5. Develop the benchmarks
	o Benchmarks are kept current as part of an overall business intelligence activity by dedicated internal assignments
	
	o Goals based on benchmarks are:
	
	   • Appropriate, and prioritized for meaningful business impact
	
	   • Achievable. If they are a stretch, ensure the tools and road map to achieve them are available
	
	o Any partnerships are nourished (and remain justified) through the exchange of useful, high-quality data

Understand the Quality and Efficiency Your Prospects Need

Lean Tools & Concepts

An important recent framework for analysis and decision-making is that of a lean operation, focused simultaneously on:

o Decreasing Waste, Cost and Cycle Time
o Increasing Capacity Potential
o Increasing Quality
o Low Absenteeism/voluntary Turnover
o Extensive Measurement of Key Processes
o High Levels of Worker Involvement, Ownership and Commitment

Elevator Pitch

"The 'Lean' philosophy focuses on the relentless elimination of waste based on a system of production as needed (a 'pull' system)."

All of these benefits, and the ability to sustain them, are derived from the disciplined application of common sense tools and techniques that have been developed and refined in the manufacturing environment since the early 20th Century (see the chart on the next page for some of the heritage). For most traditional organizations lean requires a significant culture change, with executives and managers directly involved and floor personnel empowered and trained for continuous improvement.

The 'mass production' of transactions, documents, paper instruments, and records has created the need for lean operations in the clerical world ('Lean Office'), where higher quality translates into both operating efficiency and (often more importantly) improved effectiveness with highly leveraged benefits.

To speak intelligently about Lean, you should know the following definitions:

5S Principles	In Japanese: seiri, seiton, seiso, seiketsu, and shitsuke. In English: sort, straighten, sweep, standardize, and sustain. Lean production with Six Sigma quality is not possible in a disorganized, dirty workplace. In a lean audit, the 5S exercise is a very good starting point
Agile Development	Rapid, iterative design of products enabled by small, independent teams with powerful software tools in order to rapidly respond to market opportunities
Chaku-Chaku	A production approach that automates a sequence of steps from machine to machine, minimizing the opportunity for human error
Constraint Management	Every production line has a 'drum' – a process that constrains and sets the pace for the whole factory
Daily Focus on Lean	Every work group needs a very brief stand-up huddle every day to ensure a coordinated effort. They also need an easy visual reference throughout the work day to stay focused on the critical objectives of the group
Muda	Japanese for 'waste.' Lists of typical types of office and manufacturing waste can act as checklists for identifying the most common causes
Kanban	Kanban means 'storefront' and refers to the practice of treating production centers as standalone store-like demand centers, to pull inventory through a production process
Lean Accounting	Standard cost accounting typically focuses on valuing inventory at all stages of production, and on keeping expensive machinery in production. Lean accounting instead focuses on value created in the overall value stream, and in optimizing the inventory even if key machines are occasionally idle
Line Balancing	A production line is balanced when each process step takes about the same amount of time, and less than Takt time
Overall Equipment Effectiveness	OEE provides insights into the effectiveness of production equipment by measuring output versus capacity
Poka Yoke	Poka-yoke is applied to methods, equipment, systems, and processes to make errors difficult or impossible to make. For example, stamping presses generally have safety gates and two-hand operating triggers to keep operators from reaching into a closing press
Pull Philosophy	Pull systems attempt to produce goods only when needed and bring them to where they are needed

Single Minute Exchange of Die	SMED refers to a disciplined approach to reducing machine setup time to the absolute minimum to support optimum operating flexibility and machine run time.
Spaghetti Diagram	An illustration of the actual physical flow of materials through a production process in order to design the most effective and efficient flow
Standardized Work	Describes an individual worker's job as a series of defined steps, producing specific WIP quantities in as close to Takt time as possible
Takt Time	The available production time divided by the rate of customer demand. For example, if customers demand 480 automobiles per 480 minute shift, Takt time is one minute
Throughput	The amount of product coming off the assembly line in a given period
Total Productive Maintenance	TPM merges the preventive maintenance schedule into the production schedule to minimize planned and unplanned down time
Value Stream Map	A display of all of the steps required to deliver a product from raw material to customer delivery, and focuses especially on barriers to a smooth and timely flow
Visual Workplace	Visual cues can make it dramatically easier for workers to maintain a safe, efficient workplace
Yield	The percentage of good product coming out of an operation compared to the input resources

Six Sigma Quality Concepts

Elevator Pitch

"Six Sigma refers to the sixth standard deviation from the mean of a normal curve, applied to production to mean about 3.4 errors per million parts produced – very high quality indeed. The term has also been extended in popular usage to refer to a program with a defined tool kit designed to produce Six Sigma quality."

W. Edward Deming was the production statistician who developed the quantitative tools and techniques that reset quality expectations across industries worldwide. After established U.S. and European industries rejected his statistical process methods in the 1950's, Japanese manufacturers adopted his concepts and captured a significant share of world markets in automobiles, electronics, and other consumer goods before other regional markets could react. Following the Japanese lead, many consulting organizations, internal and external, have developed tool kits for continuously improving business processes.

W. Edward Deming [3]

With a major commitment to defense against foreign competition in the early 1980's, Motorola developed particularly successful practices to systematically improve processes by eliminating defects, and trademarked the term 'Six Sigma' to refer to its system. General Electric's implementation of 'Six Sigma' features definable, repeatable processes executed by dedicated professional 'green belts' and 'black belts.'

Mathematically, 'Six Sigma' refers to six standard deviations from the mean of a normal curve (a mathematical tool for analyzing variances). A process that achieves or exceeds a Six Sigma level of quality will by definition have 3.4 errors, or fewer, per million. Like lean production in the prior chapter, Six Sigma is a philosophy, in this case dedicated to delivering consistently the quality customers demand.

Some organizations have attempted to apply the Six Sigma concepts and toolkit to activities with relatively low throughput or non-repetitive tasks. In such cases it is better, when errors are unacceptably expensive, to use the error-proofing tools of lean rather than the process control tools of Six Sigma. The following terms will help you speak intelligently about Six Sigma.

Total Quality Management	TQM applies statistical methods to ensure quality standards are met wherever products are made, throughout an organization
Statistical Process Controls	SPC charts track key metrics in production to provide early warning when processes begin making out-of-spec products
ISO 9000	The International Standards organization has created a number of ISO standards for how a company should operate to create products of consistent quality. These standards have been widely accepted, and ISO 9000 certification is important for marketing across a broad spectrum of complex products
Baldrige Award	An annual award created by the U.S. government to recognize organizations with quality and performance excellence that added to America's competitiveness in an increasingly competitive world market
Normal Distribution	The Bell Curve is a foundational concept of statistics, applicable to a broad range of natural phenomena. It demonstrates that the frequency of any measurement decreases predictably as the distance from the mean increases
Quality Function Deployment	QFD is a tool used by a cross-functional team to address and coordinate product development to ensure right-first-time performance and on-going success
Histograms	Histograms depict the frequency of measurements along a continuum. A very large sample becomes a Bell Curve
Xbar Charts	Xbar charts track multiple samples in production to help determine whether errors are due to random events or to special causes that can be corrected
Design of Experiments	Design of experiments (DOE) is the design of manipulation, observation and analysis procedures where variation (in product quality, for example) is present to determine the causes of variation

Apply the Tools to Get It Done

The tools used to correct efficiency problems (lean elimination of waste) and to correct effectiveness problems (Six Sigma production of products that meet customer requirements) are essentially the same, and require the same planning, teamwork and executive sponsorship to succeed.

Regardless of which type of problem is being addressed, the tools are used in a logical sequence, as follows:

> ### Elevator Pitch
>
> "Lean and Six Sigma use the same tools, and both disciplines require the same planning, teamwork, and sponsorship."

1. Identify the Problem

Brainstorming	1. Get as many ideas as possible 2. There are no silly or bad ideas 3. Everyone joins in 4. Hitchhiking (building on another's ideas) is okay 5. here are no judgments or discussions of ideas while ideas are being generated
Day in the Life Of (DILO) Studies	When you need to know what REALLY goes on, follow the person who does it around and record everything he or she does
Process Flow Analysis	Processes, not people, cause the majority of operating problems. Process flow analysis is a good place to start identifying production quality or efficiency improvement opportunities
Ratio Delay Analysis	Ratio Delay Analysis provides a quick view of shop floor activity, based on a number of short observations, in order to identify improvement opportunities

2. Analyze the Problem

Affinity Diagram	The Affinity Diagram helps teams focus by organizing ideas into logically related categories
Ishikawa Diagram	An Ishikawa (or 'root cause') diagram logically connects a problem to its roots in an intuitive 'fish bone' format

3. Prioritize Actions to Fix the Problem

Failure Modes and Effects Analysis (FMEA)	FMEA attempts to prioritize problem elimination actions based on expert understanding of severity, probability, and difficulty to detect
Multivoting	Multivoting is a tool used to gain consensus among experts about priorities selected from a number of desirable solutions by giving each expert a number of votes to apply as they deem appropriate
Pareto Analysis	The Pareto diagram arrays problem sources according to their frequency of occurrence, demonstrating the 80—20 rule (80% of the problems stem from 20% of the causes)

4. Estimate the Challenge

Force Field Analysis	Force Field analysis considers factors that enable progress toward a goal and barriers to achieving the goal in order to develop approaches to supporting the enablers and removing the barriers
SIPOC	SIPOC is the acronym for the Supplier-Input-Process-Output-Supplier chain, analyzed to ensure key requirements and issues are understood as process improvements are designed and implemented

5. Establish a Project

Design for Six Sigma (DMADV of DFSS)	Design for Six Sigma (DFSS) is the development approach to building Six Sigma quality into a product or process at inception
DMAIC	DMAIC is the acronym for the most widely used Six Sigma operations improvement steps: define, measure, analyze, improve, and control
Generic Business Improvement Process	Failure to follow a disciplined process for business improvement practically guarantees failure to achieve the desired results. Consulting firms often create them to differentiate themselves, but they all have some form of Plan-Do-Review in them

Acceptable Quality Level (AQL)

Quality Control measures attempt to ensure that produced items are of acceptable quality before they are used, by applying complex statistical techniques in a discipline known as 'Acceptance Sampling.' Acceptance Sampling is a compromise between not doing any inspection at all and inspecting 100% of the units in each batch. The objective is to make product disposition decisions based on informed quality estimates.

The key concepts originated in World War II, when the U.S. military needed to ensure ordinance would work in the field. Of course they could not test it all, so they turned to statistical methods to determine what representative test sample would provide confidence that a batch was good.

Representative samples are selected from a population and tested to determine whether the lot is at an Acceptable Quality Level (AQL) using an 'Acceptance Plan' or 'Sampling Plan,' based either on attributes of individual discrete tested products or on statistical measures of batch variables.

These principles can be applied to most products and services acquired in volume. Software is a special case, where quality refers to two related but distinct notions, functional quality (conformance to design) and structural quality (adherence to sound architectural principles). Once it is fully tested every true copy will be as acceptable as the original, and any necessary sampling will focus primarily on the quality of the copy.

Be Financially Literate – Your Prospects Are!

Financial Concepts

Elevator Pitch

"To sell to someone who cares about financial performance absolutely requires basic financial literacy."

It is sometimes helpful to relate business financial management to something we really care about, our own personal finances. The principles are exactly the same: don't spend more than you or your company can afford and don't run out of cash. Financial success has four determinants: how much money comes in, how much goes out, what you own, and what you owe. The illustration on the next page depicts a super-simple Income Statement and Balance Sheet, with arrows indicating Cash Flow.

Financial statements have evolved over the years to show in a standard, easy to read format what a company owns and owes, whether it is making or losing money, and whether its cash flow is positive or negative.

Your prospect uses financial statements to measure his or her organization's progress and will always view the ROI business case with financial statement impacts in mind. For this reason, selling costly products or solutions requires you, the salesperson, to understand the impact on the prospect's financial statements in order to explain the financial value, cash effects, and cost justification for your offering.

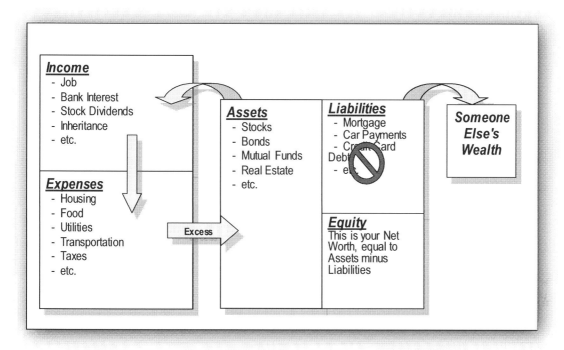

Profit & Loss (Income) Statement

The P&L (Profit and Loss) is a standard financial statement that presents revenue, costs, and the resulting profits for one or more fiscal periods. Translation: how much money came in from all sources, and how much was spent for everyday operations.

One of the most significant lines on this statement is 'gross profit,' indicating the amount earned (or lost) on each sale BEFORE any of the overhead (costs of being in business) are factored in. If your prospect is not making money on this line, he or she might be in real trouble. In that case, confirm that your solution will help, and that the prospect will be able to pay.

Typical P&L Statement

	2012	2013
Gross Sales	191,653,001	202,460,000
Less: Returns & Allowances	2,750,600	2,024,600
Net Sales	188,902,401	200,435,400
Total Materials	40,614,401	42,962,000
Total Labor	21,057,054	22,270,600
Depreciation	4,765,241	5,100,000
Other Factory Overhead	8,469,925	8,000,000
Total Cost of Goods	74,906,621	78,332,600
Gross Profit	113,995,780	122,102,800
Gross Profit Margin	60.3%	60.9%
R&D	10,737,085	9,000,000
Marketing & Sales	36,800,337	40,000,000
General & Administrative	17,694,505	18,000,000
Interest	2,365,897	2,200,000
Total Period Cost	67,597,824	69,200,000
Net Profit Before Tax	46,397,956	52,902,800
NPBT Margin	24.6%	24.9%
Tax @ 34.0%	15,775,305	17,986,952
Net Profit After Tax	30,622,651	34,915,848
NPAT Margin	16.2%	16.4%

Balance Sheet

The Balance Sheet is a standard financial statement that presents assets, liabilities, and equity at the end of a fiscal period (often a calendar year). This statement describes what is owned (assets) and who owns them (creditors own the liabilities and the company owns the equity [Net Worth]). Balance refers to the fact that Assets are exactly equaled (balanced) by Liabilities and Equity - every penny of asset value has an owner. The balance sheet also identifies which assets and liabilities are current (cash will flow within one year) and which are not likely to change in that time period (fixed assets and long-term debt, such as mortgages).

Typical Balance Sheet

ASSETS		LIABILITIES	
Cash & Securities	31,377,349	Accounts Payable	34,179,563
Accounts Receivable	34,798,632	Other Current Liabilities	12,000,000
Inventories	14,755,694		
Other Current Assets	2,983,651		
Total Current Assets	**83,915,326**	**Total Current Liabilities**	**46,179,563**
Factory, Machinery & Equipment	109,763,552	Bank Notes	32,500,000
Less: Depreciation	(63,850,994)	Other Long Term Liabilities	
Net Fixed Assets	45,912,558		
Other Assets		**Total Liabilities**	**46,179,563**
		Paid in Capital	20,000,000
		Retained Earnings	63,648,321
		Stockholders Equity	**83,648,321**
Total Assets	**129,827,884**	**Total Liabilities & Equity**	**129,827,884**

Cash Flow or Funds Flow

The 'Cash Flow', or 'Funds Flow,' or 'Sources and Uses' is a standard financial statement that shows how cash was obtained and used in a fiscal period. Cash can flow when:

o   An excess of earnings minus expenses flows into assets (as cash)
o   Assets are purchased for cash (equal to the value of assets purchased)
o   Assets are sold for cash
o   Liabilities are increased (for example, cash can be borrowed from the bank)
o   Liabilities are decreased (for example, cash can be paid back)
o   Equity is increased (cash from investors)
o   Equity is decreased (dividends or stock repurchases)

Often, balance sheet changes are not cash transactions but will affect the Cash Flow Statement. For example, vendors may 'lend' in the form of raw materials. Nonetheless, this shows up on the Cash Flow Statement as cash from a Source (the vendor liability) and cash to a Use (raw material inventory).

From your prospect's perspective, cash is a big deal, as suggested by the old adage, "when you are out of cash, you are out of business." Most companies expend significant energy to design and enforce appropriate controls with supporting metrics to ensure reliable cash flow, and you will need to understand these in order to help your prospect buy. For example, you might lease or finance a sale to help a buyer manage the period impact of the purchase.

Cash flow related to software acquisition can be particularly creatively managed, through a subscription model known as 'Software as a Service' (SaaS) which rents services as needed, or through the 'Cloud,' where payment might be up-front or as-you-go. The many on-premises and hosting site options can significantly affect the timing and controllability of IT-related cash flow.

Typical Cash Flow Statement

SOURCES AND USES

Profit After Tax	30,622,651
Depreciation	4,765,241
Changes in Receivables	75,600
Changes in Inventories	75,601
Changes in Accounts Payable	455,002
Changes in Other Assets/Liabilities	
Net Cash From/To Operations	**35,994,095**
Changes in Fixed Assets	
Sale or Purchase of a Business	
Net Cash From/To Investments	-
Changes in Notes Payable	
Changes in Paid-In-Capital	
Dividends	(24,000,000)
Net Cash From/To Financing	**(24,000,000)**
Net Cash Flow	**11,994,095**

Key Ratios

Various ratios are computed and widely used to evaluate financial strengths and weaknesses, and trends, of a company. The ratios shown are typical, and can be characterized as Activity, Leverage/Solvency, Liquidity, Market Value, Productivity, and Profitability Ratios. Their use depends on the specific concerns of executives, managers, and shareholders. It can be misleading to use such ratios without a context, such as industry norms or period to period comparisons, and few reliable ratio benchmarks exist at levels of granularity meaningful to operating managers, but the higher level ratios in the ratio categories that follow can provide guidance.

Because they are intuitive and fact-based, ratios can provide metrics useful in measuring the gaps that your solution will address. Be sure to select the ones that really matter to your prospect.

Commonly Used Ratios

Liquidity

Working Capital	= Current Assets - Current Liabilities
EBIT	= Pre-Tax Profit + Interest Expense
Current Ratio	= Current Assets / Current Liabilities
Acid Test	= (Current Assets - Inventories) / Current Liabilities
Free Cash Flow	= Period Cash Flow + Dividends + Interest - Tax on Interest

Activity

Days Sales Outstanding	= 365 x A/R / Revenue (Annualized)
Days of Supply	= 365 x Inventory / Cost of Goods Sold (Annualized)
Operating Cycle	= Days Sales Outstanding + Days of Supply
Inventory Turns	= Cost of Goods Sold (Annualized) / Inventory
Asset Leverage	= Revenue (Annualized) / Total Assets
Cash Flow vs Earnings	= Period Cash Flow / Period Profit After Tax

Leverage (Solvency, Long-Term Debt)

Debt Ratio	= Total Liabilities / Total Assets
Debt / Equity Ratio	= Total Liabilities / Equity
Interest Coverage	= Earnings Before Interest and Taxes (EBIT) / Interest Expense

Profitability

Gross Profit Margin	= Gross Profit / Revenue
Profit Margin	= Profit After Tax / Revenue
Pre-Tax Profit Margin	= Pre-Tax Profit / Revenue
Return on Assets	= Profit After Tax / Total Assets
Return on Invested Capital	= Profit After Tax / Equity

Market Value

Price / Earnings Ratio	= Market Value of Stock / Profit After Tax
Dividend Yield	= Dividends / Market Value of Stock
Dividend Payout	= Dividends / Profit After Tax

Productivity

Revenue / Employee	= Revenue / Internal Headcount
Profit / Employee	= Profit After Tax / Internal Headcount

Liquidity Ratios

These ratios provide insight into whether an organization can pay its bills.

- *Current Ratio*: Current Assets divided by Current Liabilities, a measure of liquidity, or the ability to pay current debts out of current assets
- *Cash Ratio*: Cash divided by current liabilities (measures the ability to pay current obligations with cash)
- *Acid Test*: (AKA Quick Ratio) An extreme version of the Current Ratio, the 'Acid Test' assumes Inventory cannot be converted to cash
- *EBITDA*: (Earnings before Interest, Taxes, Depreciation, and Amortization) is a measure commonly used by investors to understand a company's ability to incur and service debt
- *EBIT*: Pre-Tax Profit plus Interest Expense
- *Free Cash Flow:* Cash available to pay to owners and lenders, calculated by subtracting Dividends and After Tax Interest from Net Cash Flow for a period
- *Working Capital*: Capital tied up in Current Assets (such as Cash, Accounts Receivable and Inventories) less Current Liabilities (such as Accounts Payable).

Activity Ratios

These ratios can indicate whether an organization is managing its work activities with financial effectiveness and efficiency.

- *Asset Leverage*: Use of assets to gain the optimum revenue (measured as Revenue divided by Assets).
- *Cash Flow versus Earnings*: An indicator of liquidity trends, computed for a given period
- *Days Sales Outstanding (DSO)*: A measure of Accounts Receivable, measured as A/R divided by annual Revenue, times 365. DSO theoretically measures how many days we wait after delivering a product to get paid for it. In general, shorter cycles are better
- *Days of Supply*: The number of days' worth of inventory on hand, estimated on the basis of use rate. See also inventory turns, the reciprocal.
- *Operating Cycle*: The number of days from the time money is spent until it is collected, from the purchases that do into inventory to the collection of receivables
- *Inventory Turns*: (AKA Turnover) Turns measure how fast inventory is used and replaced. Different categories of inventory can turn at different rates. Computed as Total annual COGS divided by Inventory. Higher turns reduce invested capital

Leverage/Solvency Ratios

These ratios show the ability of an organization to get long-term cash from investors and banks.

- o *Debt / Equity Ratio*: Total Liabilities divided by Total Equity, indicates the balance of the stakes held between owners and creditors. A ratio of 1:1 suggests lenders see acceptable risk in lending an amount equal to the owners' equity
- o *Debt Ratio*: Total Liabilities divided by Total Assets, indicates how much of the company is owed to creditors
- o *Interest Coverage*: Also called Cash Coverage. Ability to meet all interest obligations out of earnings
- o *Times Interest Earned*: Earnings Before Interest and Taxes divided by Interest
- o *Total Debt Ratio*: The ratio to total assets of all debts of all maturities to all creditors

Profitability Ratios

These are key ratios indicating how efficiently a company earns money, generally compared within an industry, since different industries exhibit very different results.

- o *Gross Profit Margin*: The contribution made toward corporate expenses by the sale of products, calculated as Revenue less Cost of Goods Sold, expressed as a percentage
- o *Pre-Tax Profit Margin*: Pre-Tax Profit Margin is a percentage calculated as Net Profit before Tax divided by Revenue
- o *Profit Margin*: Profit Margin is a percentage calculated as Net Profit after Tax (NPAT) divided by Revenue
- o *Return on Assets*: This is a measure of the efficient use of assets to gain profit (NPAT divided by Total Assets). Other ratios may be more meaningful in certain circumstances, such as Return on Controllable Assets (ROCA), meaning assets under the control of the department or organization responsible for their use
- o *Return on Invested Capital (ROIC)*: This is a measure of the efficient use of assets to gain profit (NPAT divided by Equity)
- o *Total Asset Turnover*: A measure of how productive assets are at generating revenue

Market Value Ratios

These are ratios of interest to the stock market.

- *Dividend Payout*: Per cent of Net Profit after Tax paid out to shareholders in the form of Dividends or Distributions (Dividends divided by NPAT)
- *Dividend Yield*: The value of Dividends paid compared to the Market Value of a stock
- *Market-To-Book Ratio*: Current price of a share of stock divided by the accounting value of that share
- *Price/Earnings (P/E) Ratio*: The value of a stock expressed as a multiple of a company's earnings, based on expectations in the industry. This ratio is widely used to measure the stock market's enthusiasm for a stock. High multiples suggest stock buyers see more value than current earnings would suggest, based on business combinations, e-commerce, business efficiency, or other factors

Productivity Ratios

This type of ratio indicates the efficiency of an organization's use of resources in gaining financial benefits.

- *Profit / Revenue Per Employee*: This is a measure of the efficient use of human resources in securing profit or income for an organization
- *Asset Utilization Ratios*: Any ratios that measure how efficiently a firm uses its assets to generate sales
- *Average Accounting Return*: Defined as average net income divided by average book value

Talk about Finance

Return on Investment (ROI)

Return-on-Investment metrics vary widely in terms of what they measure and over what period. For example, they may look at pre-tax or after-tax profit or at cash flow returns against an out-of-pocket or otherwise measured investment, over the current year or any other appropriate time horizon.

The most popular ROI concepts are:

Return on Invested Capital (ROIC)	This is a ratio of the Profit After Taxes (PAT) to the owner's equity, measuring the quality of the investment
Net Present Value (NPV)	This is the discounted value of the future stream of cash flow associated with the investment
Internal Rate of Return (IRR)	This is the per cent rate of return that would cause the NPV to be zero, i.e., the investment exactly equal to the discounted (at the IRR rate) returns of the future
Payback	This is the length of time required to completely recover the investment

These terms are explained in detail on the next few pages.

Return on Invested Capital (ROIC)

One of the most effective metrics of this type is ROIC, measured to focus on the after-tax earnings on the average equity invested. It can be viewed for any period in the format illustrated, and provides excellent insights into how and where money is made in an organization. Its special strength comes from the viewer's ability to see instantly the effects of specific revenue, cost, and asset initiatives, and to assign accountabilities in an intuitive way. A related metric sometimes presented in a similar format is Return on Controllable Assets (ROCA), measuring the effectiveness of managers controlling specific assets.

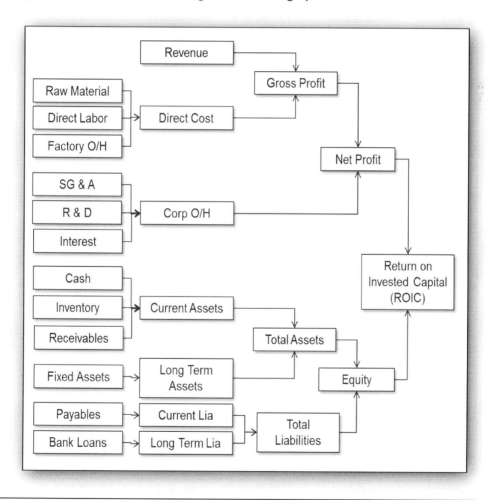

Net Present Value (NPV)

Net Present Value is a calculated estimate of the value of an investment's cash outflows and inflows over the life of the investment. It is based on the concept that money in hand at present is worth more than money in the future. Future income is 'discounted.' Bank interest reflects this reality and could be used as the discount rate – will the investment under consideration pay as much as or more than bank interest?

Elevator Pitch

"Money today is worth more than money tomorrow."

Many organizations set 'hurdle' rates as the discount rate for their investments. Every investment decision must apply that discount rate and indicate a positive NPV, earning more than the minimum return (for example, more than bank interest). In reality, the rates are typically significantly higher than bank interest because risks are often much higher than a savings bank.

To calculate NPV:

1. *PVIF = 1 / (1 + R) ^ t where PVIF is the Present Value Interest Factor for each period, R is the Interest Rate and t is the period (generally year 1, 2, 3, etc.). Each successive period will apply the interest rate to the prior year's reduced rate, so later money is realized, the less it is worth in the present.*

2. *PV = Amount x PVIF where PV is Present Value for each period and Amount refers to the amount to be realized in that period*

3. *Net Present Value (NPV) = Sum of (PV) for all periods*
   - *Assumes the cash is invested in the period prior to period 1.*
   - *Negative values in early periods represent investments*

Net Present Value Illustrated

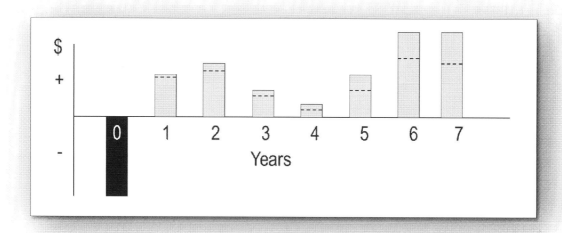

In this illustration, each successive year is discounted at a higher percentage than the year before, with a significant reduction in the value of year 7. Here is an example (not the same as illustrated above) with numbers:

	Period 0	Period 1	Period 2	Period 3	Total
Raw Value	(1,000)	400	400	400	200
Discount Factor @ 10%	1.0	.90	.81	.72	
Discounted Value	(1,000)	360	324.4	288	(27.6)

Note that in this example, the raw value looks like a $200 positive investment, but discounted at 10% (i.e., compared to investing at 10%), it has lost value.

NPV provides the cash value of an investment in today's terms but does not address whether the discount rate is appropriate or how long cash will be tied up.

Excel has a powerful NPV calculator, but it will underestimate (discount) the value of the initial investment. To correct for this, use the NPV calculator for years 2 and subsequent, then add the first year (a negative value) to calculate NPV accurately - NPV (Cell containing Year 2: Cell containing Year n) + Cell containing Year 1. Also, if you leave a period blank in Excel, it is assumed not included; if you enter a zero, it will be included.

Internal Rate of Return (IRR)

Internal Rate of Return refers to the rate of return calculated directly from the cash outflows and inflows of that project. This can be complex for fluctuating cash streams, but IRR can also be considered the Discount Rate at which NPV is equal to zero – the present value of all the inflows exactly equals the present value of all outflows.

IRR has the advantage of describing investment efficiency, but is not helpful in understanding an investment's size or timing.

As a practical matter, it would require multiple iterations of the NPV calculation to find the rate at which NPV is zero, but fortunately Excel has a powerful built in IRR function – IRR(Cell containing Year 1 : Cell containing Year n). Note that, as for the NPV function, if you leave a period blank in Excel, it is assumed not included; if you enter a zero, it will be included.

Payback Chart

One of the key metrics investors consider before committing their funds is payback, or how long until the income covers the outgo. This can be viewed on a pre-tax or after-tax basis, or based on cash flow, and it can be viewed on a raw or discounted basis. The payback chart illustrated here is based on raw cash flow, and shows a lot more than payback. By showing the cumulative cash flow over time it provides a sense of the timing, amount, and risks, and it helps set expectations against which to measure the actual results.

Elevator Pitch

"Investors are generally concerned about when they will get their money back. The Payback Chart sets expectations not only for when, but about the deepest point and the attractiveness over time."

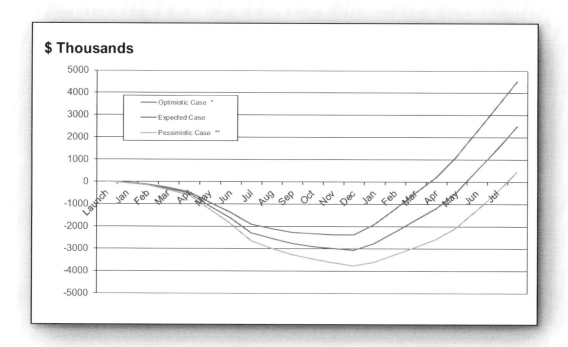

Breakeven Chart

Elevator Pitch

"For a new business or a new product, it is critical to know how many units must be sold to avoid losing money."

It is useful to know, when revenues are uncertain, exactly how much must be sold to break even (not lose money). Some costs related to each sale are Variable – they vary in direct proportion to the number of units sold. For example, the material used in each item has the same cost within a reasonable volume range (beyond that range, volume pricing breaks and other factors can impact the cost). Other costs are Fixed – unchanged by volume. For instance, factory rent is not changed for higher throughput (again up to a point – more space may be needed as significant increases occur).

Breakeven Analysis involves computation of the point at which profit contribution exactly equals the fixed costs of a company. This is usually shown on a graph and used to further estimate how much profit or loss will be experienced above and below the breakeven revenue (or volume) point.

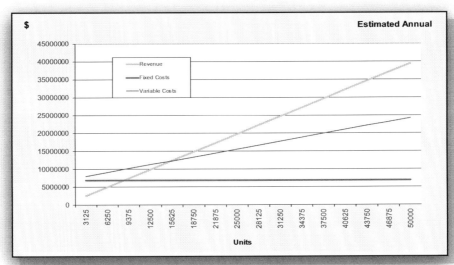

Breakeven Units = Fixed Cost / (Unit Price - Unit Cost)

Insourcing and Outsourcing

In his excellent book "The World is Flat," Thomas Friedman notes that work of all types, and especially knowledge work, can be done anywhere on earth. In this world market what matters is quality and efficiency, and both are optimized in well-run organizations that have critical mass – sufficient sales volume to utilize their capacity and fund their continuous improvement programs. Insourcing (bringing work in-house that is currently performed by outside vendors) and outsourcing (finding reliable vendors to replace or supplement in-house capacity) are an important piece of the competitive equation.

> ## Elevator Pitch
>
> "In our flat world competitors win by producing quality goods efficiently anywhere. If you can make a purchased part better (quality and efficiency) insource it. If a reliable supplier has critical mass, outsource."

Each organization is challenged to regularly review its own production methods to determine, for every cost-significant product or service component of its offering:

If made in house:
o   Are we utilizing our dedicated resources at least 65%? (Less would suggest we might not be at critical mass.)
o   Does someone do it so much better that our cost would decrease if we bought outside? (Remember to factor in the cost of poor quality!)
o   Is this a critical core competence or scarce commodity that we can't afford to lose for its significant competitive advantage?

If Purchased:
o   Do we have underutilized resources that could be applied efficiently to this component?
o   Can we do it well enough that our cost would decrease if we made it inside?
o   Is this a critical core competence or scarce commodity that we need to better control for its significant competitive advantage?

Price Sensitivity

Elevator Pitch

"There is an optimum price point for every product. Priced above that point, fewer customers will buy and sales volume will be degraded, driving down revenue and potentially increasing unit cost. Below that point, increased demand will not cover the revenue lost."

Price sensitivity refers to the impact on revenue and profit resulting from increasing or decreasing prices. Raising a product's price will eliminate some buyers, for perceived value or affordability reasons, while lowering the price will have the opposite effect. These economic and psychological factors must be considered when setting or resetting prices.

Any product could provide an example: could GM build enough Corvettes if they were priced at $1,000 new and fully loaded? Could the Wall Street Journal sell a daily newspaper for $100 per copy? But in fact the actual optimum point – just the right number of customers at just the right price to maximize revenue or profit – requires careful analysis.

Shareholder Value

There are many ways to measure and estimate Shareholder Value, but we offer a simple view: Shareholder value is market value of the company's stock divided by the book value of the company, representing the premium stock purchasers are willing to pay for the assets of the company under its current management.

This model is based on a series of managed leverages, multiplied together, indicating how well the operating team sells and produces for a profit, how well the executive team deploys assets to drive revenue, how well the financial team uses borrowed money to gain financial leverage, and how well the CEO and PR team sell the company to the equity markets.

Elevator Pitch

"Shareholder Value can be measured by the premium over book value that people will pay to own a company's stock."

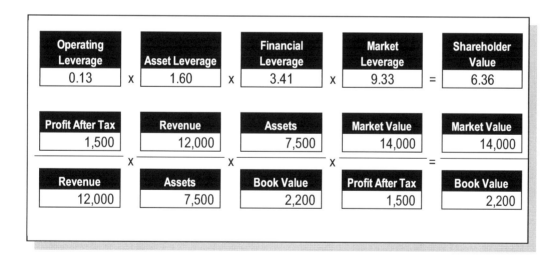

Operating Leverage		Asset Leverage		Financial Leverage		Market Leverage		Shareholder Value
0.13	x	1.60	x	3.41	x	9.33	=	6.36

Profit After Tax		Revenue		Assets		Market Value		Market Value
1,500		12,000		7,500		14,000		14,000
	x		x		x		=	
Revenue		Assets		Book Value		Profit After Tax		Book Value
12,000		7,500		2,200		1,500		2,200

Executive Highlights

Executives are apt to ask for nearly any format of any analysis outcome, for decision making or for reports to shareholders, but a few reports are most commonly used, and highlights are typically drawn from them, as in the example below. The reports are:

o   Profit & Loss Statement (P&L), showing income, costs and profits or losses by month, quarter, or year.

o   Balance Sheet, showing all assets, liabilities, and equity by month, quarter, or year.

o   Cash Flow Statement, showing the sources and uses of cash by month, quarter, or year.

o   Payback Curve, showing the cumulative inflows and outflows of cash by month in the best, worst, and expected cases. This report often includes Net Present Value (NPV) and Internal Rate of Return (IRR).

o   Return on Invested Capital breaks down costs and assets for easy analysis of the efficiency of asset use for any month, quarter, or year period.

o   Key Ratios shows some commonly calculated ratios used by accountants to assess the health of a company for any month, quarter, or year period.

o   Breakeven Chart shows the dynamics of profitability for any month, quarter, or year period.

Typical Executive Summary

Financial Highlights

$ Thousands
For the Fiscal Year Ending June 30

Racing Division
Expected Case

	2007	2008	2009	2010	2011	Total
Revenue	1,000	1,050	1,103	1,158	1,216	5,526
Gross Margin	510	540	572	605	639	2,865
Profit After Tax	240	261	278	285	321	1,384
Margin	24.0%	24.9%	25.2%	24.6%	26.4%	25.1%
Total Assets	645	832	1,036	1,222	1,443	1,443
Total Liabilities	130	131	132	133	134	134
Invested Capital	-	-	-	-	-	-
Return on Invested Capital	#DIV/0!	#DIV/0!	#DIV/0!	#DIV/0!	#DIV/0!	#DIV/0!
Net Cash Flow	209	199	168	202	237	1,015
Cumulative Cash Flow	209	408	577	778	1,015	

Executives focus on a bigger picture, uncluttered by details. Sales people do well to align their own thinking with executive thinking, and to avoid presenting complex charts full of numbers to their executive prospects.

Activity Based Costing (ABC)

Elevator Pitch

"Activity Based Costing attempts to assign costs, currently allocated, directly to the activities that drive them, suggesting products to kill or re-price or customers to drop or charge more."

Activity Based Costing (ABC) is applied when management suspects some products or customers cost more than they are worth due to customization or special handling. This problem is applicable especially to companies that use highly-allocated cost accounting methods, offer a wide variety of product configurations, and are excessively customer-driven. In such companies, special orders may drive hidden costs in marketing, engineering, production, or other departments, chewing up time and materials that may not even be in the 'Cost of Goods Sold' buckets. ABC methods attempt to track and recover some of these losses.

The analysis is done as follows:

1. Calculate unit cost from the accounting system.
2. List the main activities that drive cost, and look especially for activities that are significant cost drivers and selectively supplied to products or services.
3. Determine the units of measure and rates for the drivers.
4. Develop a database of products by customer and determine how much of the special activity was applied to each unit sold.
5. Subtract the costs from the selling price for each sale to determine its profit.
6. Sort the products and / or the customers by profit in descending order.
7. Chart each list and analyze it for gains and losses, as illustrated on the next page.

Typical ABC Analysis Result

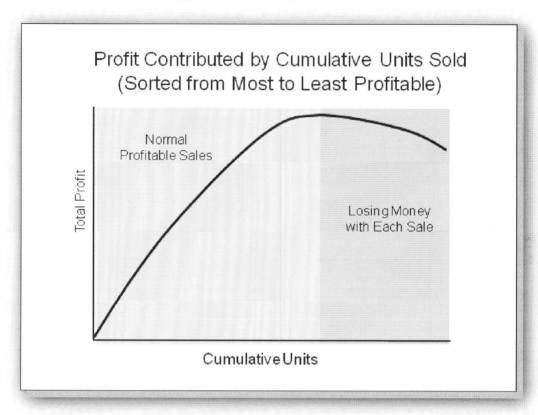

Know Today's Business Systems

Ubiquitous Systems

This chapter briefly introduces several systems that all business and sales professionals must understand.

<u>Historical Perspective</u>

Systems have evolved both in application function (software) and computing platform (hardware). Starting <u>in the 60's and 70's</u> with mainframe computers which primarily relied on hard wired software applications, these systems were physically large in size and short on flexibility and integration, but at

> ### Elevator Pitch
>
> "Virtually everyone – in any organization – touches systems. Lack of the right information in the right place at the right time can bring most organizations operations to their knees."

that time provided new found computing power for large businesses. The applications during that timeframe were mostly single applications and were rarely integrated with other applications. Most of the input for these systems came from punched cards (referred to as 80 or 96 column cards), which were punched on separate pieces of equipment. The card punch equipment had a keyboard, which operators used to type specified data which was then translated into punches on the cards. These devices were the early iteration of today's input devices (such as PCs, smart phones, and tablets). Each card and its associated punches represented some type of data such as customer numbers, names, addresses, inventory numbers and quantities, general ledger account numbers, etc. Card reading devices attached to the computers, read the data on the punched cards, translated it based on the software commands, and computed information as a part of the rudimentary software of the day.

<u>During the mid-70's and through the 80's</u>, much advancement took place in both computing (hardware) and the software used. Mainframes had more utility and mini-computers were introduced, followed quickly by personal computers (PC's). Punch card equipment was replaced by terminals (monitors wired to the computers for input). Both mini-computers and PC's were widely used by Small and Medium Businesses (SMBs). Also during this time, software became much more industry specific and integration of systems expanded dramatically. For

example, what started as a simple Accounts Receivable (AR) system grew to become an integrated financial system which included AR, Accounts Payable (AP) and General Ledger (GL). Simple inventory systems grew to integrate time phased planning and Bills of Material (BOMs), together becoming Materials Requirements Planning (MRP).

The 80's also saw the development and use of relational databases and private and public networks. The networks enabled data communication across multiple locations while the relational databases brought large volumes of data together in a logical collection system enabling improved methods of data organization, capture and reporting.

The 90's saw numerous technologies that were launched in the late 80's come into effective use, including Client / Server architectures, which took advantage of PC computing in combination with a central computer (server) in a network environment. The PC's provided both data entry and some computing at the source while being tightly coupled to the central computer (Server) which collected data via a relational database. Additionally, numerous technologies emerged such as reporting and analytics solutions for business intelligence, user interfaces, and security. During the mid-90's the Internet began to emerge for commercial use and numerous businesses began offering indexed data that was retrievable through some form of intelligent search.

At the end of the 90's, many IT initiatives shifted to software re-work to accommodate the upcoming century change. Most software developed up to that point did not accommodate a 4 digit year format but rather applied a 2 digit year, which meant going from year 99 to year 00 could throw systems into unknown or unwanted territory and calculations associated with dates would be incorrect. Worse case scenarios talked about utility grids being shut down or other infrastructures becoming inoperable as well as systems used by the hundreds of thousands of businesses worldwide not working properly. Many IT System Integration firms worked during the 90's to overcome the lurking dangers of Year 2000 (Y2K).

We got through it but Y2K concerns during the late 90's created a bit of a buying frenzy as business after business purchased new software that was guaranteed to be Y2K compliant. This was both good and bad. The good news was businesses were proactively taking action to make sure their systems were in order for the new century. The bad news was it had a crippling impact on the software industry during the early 2000's, as business software demand was non-existent for several years.

During the 2000's, use of the web (internet), digital storage, and very large data sets and everything associated with them consumed the majority of IT activity. What is termed the Digital Age began in 2002. It is a new Information Technology landscape led by web enabled applications meaning software that can be accessed using the web as the network of choice. This web as a new platform has increased the ability of businesses to reach consumers (B2C) and added a great deal of initiatives associated with B2C web solutions. A major shift has continued through the early 2000's to today in 2014 where social media, web marketing and advertising, and growth of the consumer marketplace is all about the web and smart mobile devices and applications running on any type of device. Also during the early 2000's the Sarbanes Oxley Act (SOX) was enacted by the Federal Government to enforce stricter financial reporting guidelines and ensure compliance.

On the business side, also referred to as Business to Business (B2B), major shifts in software platform options have quickly evolved providing businesses with lots of choices, such as, On-Premise (in-house), web-based, Hosted, Subscription, Software as a Service (SaaS), and the Cloud, to name a few. Businesses can now choose how to run their business software and have as much IT infrastructure as they want to manage or have managed for them. Hosted Services have become plentiful where software and the entire technical infrastructure is managed as a subscription service, thus eliminating or minimizing the amount of technical resources (hardware, network, security, personnel, etc.) a given organization needs to invest in and manage for themselves. Perceived downside is loss of control. Software as a Service (SaaS) and Cloud-based services have become common where software can be subscribed to and paid on a period basis (monthly, quarterly, etc.). All subscription models have significant revenue recognition implications for sellers using this type of software model.

2011-2014 has seen Mobile, Big Data and Cloud solutions dominate as three of the top B2B IT initiatives.

All of the advanced and flexible computing concepts where computing is made to appear everywhere and anywhere via any type of device is referred to as ubiquitous computing. In contrast to desktop computing, ubiquitous computing can occur using any device (desktops, laptops, tablets, smart phones, etc.), in any location, and in any format.

Also referred to as pervasive computing, this advanced, flexible use of technology is expanding capabilities in applications. Technologies such as artificial intelligence, location-awareness, GPS, and machine to machine intelligence are driving new value and productivity gains in solutions we touch as consumers and as business people.

In this chapter is additional background on:

o Material Requirements Planning (MRP I) and Manufacturing Resource Planning (MRP II)
o Enterprise Resource Planning
o Supply Chain Management; Collaborative Planning; Forecasting and Replenishment
o Customer Relationship Management (CRM)
o Small and Mid-Size Business Solutions (SMB)
o Social Media

Material / Manufacturing Resource Planning (MRP)

Material requirements planning (MRP) is concerned primarily with manufacturing materials while further evolved Manufacturing resource planning (MRP II) addresses operational planning (units) and financial planning (dollars), and has a 'what-if' simulation capability. These are implemented with modular software linked to a central database of business data and information for the purpose of using human and material resources more productively.

Prior to and with early computers, paper-based information systems and non-integrated systems led to numerous information errors (missing, outdated, redundant and un-reconciled data, data incorrectly keyed in, manual miscalculations) resulting in poor decisions. Also, different functional areas used incompatible databases, significantly degrading decision-making information.

In the 1980s, to facilitate 'error free' material movement, manufacturers developed early MRP systems for calculating the resource requirements of a production run based on demand forecasts. The size and complexity of the databases dictated the use of computers, originally using custom software programs that ran on mainframes.

In the 1990s, MRPII systems linked more supply chain, financial, and human resources information and production management capability into MRP databases and algorithms. Drawing on a master production schedule, MRPII produces detailed labor and machine production schedules coordinated with machine and labor capacity, linking materials movement to production runs. Data about the cost of production, including machine time, labor time and materials used, as well as final production numbers, may be provided to accounting and finance in real time.

MRP II systems can provide:
o   Better control of inventories
o   Improved scheduling
o   More efficient and effective collaboration with suppliers
o   Improved quality control for design / engineering
o   Reduced working capital through less inventory and quicker deliveries

Supply Chain Software and Collaborative Planning, Forecasting and Replenishment (CPFR)

Elevator Pitch

"CPFR removes waste from every part of the supply chain by managing supply and demand for all partners storing and delivering goods."

Step-by-Step

Wal-Mart approaches its CPFR effort following this approach:

1. Develop Front End Agreement
2. Create the Joint Business Plan
3. Create the Sales Forecast
4. Identify Exceptions for Sales Forecast
5. Resolve/Collaborate on Exception Items
6. Create Order Forecast
7. Identify Exceptions for Order Forecast
8. Resolve/Collaborate on Exception Items
9. Order Generation

Supply chains move every raw material, part, and product on earth to their point of use. This is a monstrously complex set of tasks involving millions of people, billions of daily transactions, and billions of dollars of equipment, and raises continuous, enormous challenges.

Enter the computer, and supply chain management software (SCMS), a whole range of software tools that plan and execute supply chain transactions. SCMS is often modular but modules often work seamlessly together to:

1. Process customer requirements (for successive customers along the value adding chain)
2. Process purchase orders
3. Manage inventories in storage or transit
4. Help manage suppliers
5. Apply forecasting tools to the supply / demand equations

SCMS integration solutions allow organizations to trade with their partners electronically, moving goods and money with highly leveraged human oversight.

The current state of the art is known as 'Collaborative Planning, Forecasting and Replenishment' (CPFR), a concept that enhances supply chain integration by continuously updating inventory and projected demand, making the end-to-end supply chain process more efficient. The benefits of the improved efficiency in merchandising, inventory investment, logistics, and transportation are shared by all trading partners. CPFR began as a 1995 'Open Source' initiative co-led by Wal-Mart's executives and the Cambridge, Massachusetts software and strategy firm, Benchmarking Partners, turning Wal-Mart warehousing and delivery systems into competitive weapons.

Enterprise Resource Planning (ERP) Systems

Enterprise resource planning (ERP) is the planning of how business resources (materials, employees, customers etc.) are acquired and employed. An ERP system is a business support system that maintains in a single database the data needed for a variety of business functions such as Manufacturing, Supply Chain Management, Financials, Projects, Human Resources and Customer Relationship Management.

An ERP system is based on a common database used by modular software. The common database can allow every department of a business to store and retrieve information in real-time reliably, and easily. 'Modular' implies that a business can select the modules they need, mix and match modules from different vendors, and add new modules of their own to improve business performance.

Ideally, the data for the various business functions are integrated, but in practice ERP systems often comprise a set of discrete applications, each maintaining a discrete data store within one physical database.

The initials ERP originated as an extension of MRP (material requirements planning, and then manufacturing resource planning) and CIM (computer-integrated manufacturing) and were introduced by research and analysis firm Gartner.

ERP systems now attempt to cover all basic functions of an enterprise, regardless of the organization's business or charter. Non-manufacturing businesses, non-profit organizations and governments now all use ERP systems.

To be considered an ERP system, a software package must provide the function of at least two systems. For example, a software package that provides both payroll and accounting functions could technically be considered an ERP software package. The example illustrated on the next page contains most of the core functions of an ERP. Other functions critical to a specific company, such as product configurators and customer management tools, are often bolted on.

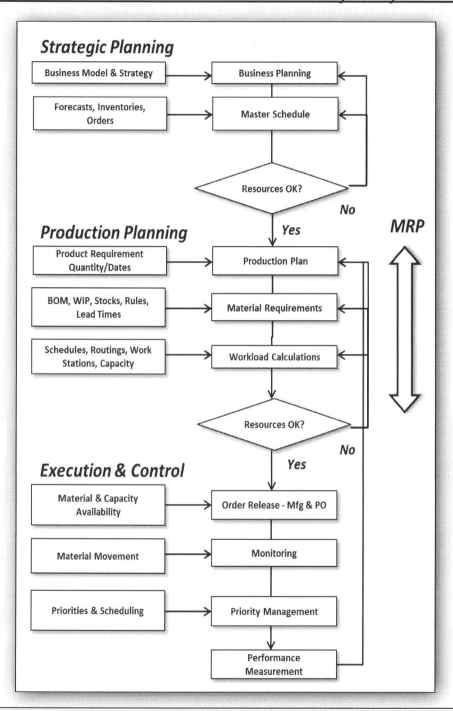

Customer Relationship Management (CRM)

Customer Relationship Management is a concept that has been around for a while. Initially starting as Sales Force Automation (SFA), which provided sales people access to some customer and prospect information, CRM has developed a variety of new and powerful tools and capabilities to help not only sales people but their entire organizations by providing instant access to such customer records and information as:

- o   Name, address, phone, e-mail
- o   Demographic data
- o   Shopping history and preferences
- o   Billing department information
- o   Customer service records
- o   Records of all significant contacts
- o   Historical information
- o   Insights into the customer's industry

CRM systems have evolved into integrated and robust solutions, critical to an enterprise's success, used extensively by accountants, product planners, production and supply chain organizations, sales teams, and marketers.

Small and Mid-Size Business Solutions (SMB)

Working in a SMB business today almost always requires significant computer skills. The typical minimum requirement is familiarity with Microsoft's Office Suite, CRM (Customer Relationship Management) solutions, and SMB business financial solutions such as MS Dynamics Suite, QuickBooks, or NetSuite, all essential to business analysis in many environments. Skills with CADCAM (Computer Aided Design / Computer Aided Manufacturing) and other task-specific software are also required in many industries.

To appreciate the challenge of information management in a small business, consider that it must perform affordably many of the functions to which large businesses apply their ERP systems and supply chain software.

Social Media

Every business is affected by social media and social networking, whether intentional or not. Facebook, LinkedIn, Twitter, and numerous other Internet sites allow conversations to develop on any topic, including discussions about product ratings and service quality, with significant potential impact on marketing and organizational reputation.

Given the unstoppable nature of social networking, It is useful to incorporate its power into marketing plans, attempting to control corporate and product images. The most obvious starting point is to identify the sites that potential buyers / supporters visit and rely on, and mount appropriate content. The most effective campaigns demonstrate expertise and generate an audience that may grow by word of mouth.

NOTE: Beyond business use, individuals, too, are affected by social media and do well to think through their personal 'brand.' Careless words and embarrassing photographs can 'go viral' (take on a life of their own) surprisingly quickly.

Consider Your Customer's Feelings

About Change Management

Figuring out what to do may be the easy part of making and implementing good decisions – such as buying your product. People don't like to change what they do or how they do it until they are convinced it is more effective and efficient and won't negatively impact the quality of their work life. Most people want to do a good job, but are hampered by weak business models, management systems, and processes. In this chapter we will describe some concepts and techniques for building enthusiasm for change - the right change.

Elevator Pitch

"This is the human side of improving a business and it is every bit as difficult as reading minds. Unless you are clairvoyant, get help!"

'Low-Hanging Fruit,' 'Quick Wins,' and 'Silver Bullets'

Elevator Pitch

"Quick wins are possible if you are standing in your own way, but there is no such thing as a free lunch."

If a process has evolved rapidly from a small operation into something more, it is possible there will be opportunities to harvest low-hanging fruit or gain quick wins (rapid improvements with high visibility and little effort). In these cases, any change effort should start there, and successes should be publicized to build momentum for change.

But some executives and managers have a tendency to look for 'silver bullets,' quick and inexpensive solutions that magically improve things dramatically. This wishful thinking can cause them to avoid the hard (and sometimes expensive) work that gains real results.

Companies should expect to work hard to make improvements, and they won't be disappointed. They may, in fact, be occasionally delighted to achieve something relatively easily. But when that happens they shouldn't congratulate themselves too enthusiastically. It just means they've been doing it really inefficiently.

When you're selling to overly optimistic prospects, be sure to help them understand the whole process your solution entails. Avoid becoming the scape goat for buyer's remorse.

Sales 'Due Diligence' Questions

While deciding to buy your product, executives are probably asking questions such as the following. Do you have the answers?

> ### Elevator Pitch
>
> "Resolve any issues raised in due diligence before attempting to sell. Always stack the deck for success."

- o What is the rationale for the action?
- o Who will be responsible for getting the work done?
- o Who must be consulted before deciding or launching major changes?
- o Who must be informed to make it work?
- o What kind of information does your organization share in making decisions and coordinating its teams? How much openness is appropriate? How will you ensure confidentiality of critical information?
- o For new products, can you demonstrate convincingly that there is an adequate market? Are customers willing to pay the prices you've assumed, in the volumes you've assumed?
- o Do you have hard evidence - i.e., direct experience or solid industry data - that your cost and asset structures are reasonable?
- o What are the risks of being wrong on any element? Have you quantified and mitigated those risks adequately?

Critical Success Factors

Facts - Emotions - Politics

The success or failure of every change depends on how accurately the facts are perceived, how painful or pleasant the change will be, and how well it addresses the political positioning of all affected parties. This is a very complex aspect of business improvement, and closely related to two other significant success factors:

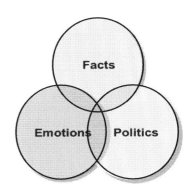

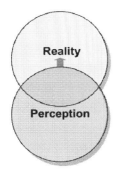

Perception vs. Reality

To be effective, a program must be fact-based and everyone with a significant role must be aligned. The view of current effectiveness must be accurately perceived, and the vision of the future must be realistic and fully embraced. Lack of alignment on the facts or their significance will stack the deck for failure.

Scope Creep & Analysis Paralysis

Projects of all types suffer from scope creep and analysis paralysis, generally driven by managers who lack experience with effective change programs. Scope creep refers to expanding the project to include organizational or process elements not originally included, and can be prevented by careful consideration of the analysis boundaries before launch. Analysis paralysis refers to expanding the data to cover every possible event, regardless of its material significance.

It is critical to consider these factors explicitly in planning any change. Many projects fail, often because these success factors were not adequately addressed.

The Soft Part is the Hard Part

The human side of creating valuable and lasting change is often more difficult than figuring out what to do, or even finding the money. The critical success factors described on the previous page are interrelated and require judgment and insight to apply masterfully. When in doubt, listen carefully. When not in doubt, listen even more carefully.

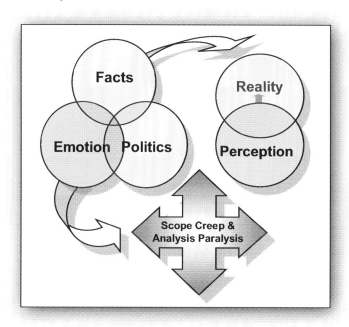

Consider Your Customer's Feeling

Are They Ready for Change?

Organizational culture will determine the success or failure of a change program. Some organizations isolate and destroy change agents and reject anything new; others are more adaptive. This quick survey provides a high-level view of change determinants. Few organizations will exhibit all of the tendencies at either the left (overly conservative) or the right (overly flexible) end of the scale, but a realistic view will help in positioning a change program for success. This survey appears in the available CD-ROM Surveys file, and a typical result chart appears on the next page.

"Rate your prospect along the following dimensions:"

	1	2	3	4	5	
All Talk						All Action
Complacent						Too Impatient
Too Frugal						Wasteful
Rigid Planning						Ad Hoc
Profit Compelled						Customer Compelled
Rigid Standards						Inconsistency
Data Driven						Instinct Driven
Non-learning						Fad Driven
Bureaucratic						Unstructured
Too People Orientation						Too Task Oriented
Hero Dependent						Overuse of Teams
Too Much Consensus						Dictatorship
Homogeneity						Detrimental Diversity
Functional Silos						Process Tunnels

Change Readiness Index

An organization with a healthy culture will tend to fall in the center of this Culture Profile chart, with few extreme traits. Extreme traits, when they do appear, need to be addressed to ensure the success of an improvement project. In fact, extreme traits may be detrimental in day-to-day operations and may be worthy of a change program in their own right.

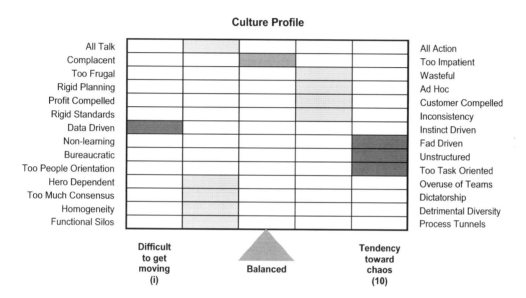

Culture Profile

Implementation of change is always a challenge, regardless of the clarity of the problem and its solution.

Are They Ready to Buy? Communicating and Reading Communication

Sales Tip

Make it a point to understand body language and buying behavior and be sensitive to it in all face to face meetings. It can help you determine "on the fly", if changes are necessary to ensure a positive outcome.

Communication in a selling situation with a prospective customer or in any type of business meeting is about much more than the words you speak and the words you hear. There is a considerable body of literature describing physiological receptivity signals. Looking for and identifying body language of a prospective customer or business associates you are presenting to may make the difference between getting buy-in or not.

Without tuning in to body language, in a face-to-face meeting, there is the potential that you exit without a proper understanding of what just took place.

Make Contact
When a prospective customer is speaking to you, he or she wants to feel that you are listening and his feelings are validated. Just nodding your head slightly sends a message that you are listening and in agreement. You can build on such non-verbal expression throughout the course of your interactions.

Control Your Hands
Limit how much you use hand gestures in meetings with prospective customers. Most well-spoken sales people are able to communicate without excessive gesticulation. Subtle hand gestures are fine and occasional strong gestures might be appropriate (depending on the situation).

Body-Language
Notice how the prospective customer is standing or sitting. Are his or her arms crossed? Is he or she leaning forward or backward? According to the article

Consider Your Customer's Feeling

'Harnessing The Power Of Body Language In Selling' by Art Siegel, a prospective customer who is interested in what you have to say may lean forward with arms uncrossed, showing he / she is open to what you are saying. A prospective customer who has crossed arms or legs might be saying that he or she is not fully embracing what you are trying to convey. These are not absolute indicators, but may help you know where you stand.

When Speaking, Position Yourself

Position yourself at about a 45-degree angle so that you are leaning in toward the prospective customer as you speak. By leaning in and directing your body toward him or her you show that you are fully focused.

Make and Keep Eye Contact

A prospective customer is unlikely to trust a salesperson who is not making eye contact. There is no need to look directly into the eyes of the prospect every moment that he or she is speaking or every time that you speak, but keeping consistent and sufficient eye contact reinforces the message that you have nothing to hide.

The Emotional Cycle of Change

Major purchases can generate strong feelings, sometimes even sufficient to cripple a program and generate disappointing results. It is a primary job of the buyer – with help from the seller – to anticipate and counter the emotions, to ensure the product is implemented successfully.

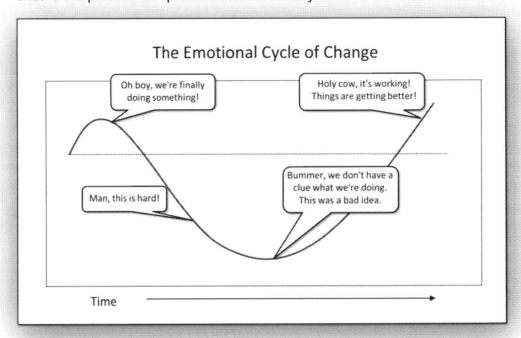

At the outset, assuming the organization sees the program as positive and exciting; there will be unrealistic expectations for the new 'silver bullet.' Buyers need to help the organization anticipate the battle ahead realistically. Next, when the hard work of change begins, leaders should focus the organization on the long-term benefits, and how much better life will be with the improvements. In large product installations, people are often worn down by hard work and limited near-term results. So in the middle of an installation, the buyers need to be cheerleaders, providing for early wins and interim rewards to maintain the focus. As improvements sink into daily work, organizations tend to become a little manic. It is important to celebrate the progress, but also to provide a sense of reality: the need for continuous improvement is continuous.

Consider Your Customer's Feeling

In general, people act when they are moved emotionally to act. No matter how rational your product or solution is, no matter how strong your business case, you need to ensure that your prospective customer has the initial enthusiasm to get started.

Then you need to ensure that enthusiasm is renewed as challenges and setbacks arise during installation / implementation. You are not immune to the Emotional Cycle of Change, either, but brace yourself with the knowledge that these challenges provide an outstanding customer relationship opportunity. When your ideas and thought leadership lead through adversity to success, you will become your customer's trusted ally.

Index

Index

Sources

1. Crosby, Philip, *Quality Is Free: The Art of Making Quality Certain*, 1980, Mentor Press, Seattle, WA
2. Beck, Kent, et al. (2001), "Manifesto for Agile Software Development," Agile Alliance. http://agilemanifesto.org/
3. W. Edward Deming. This photo is copyrighted (or assumed to be copyrighted) and unlicensed. It is believed that the use of this work to illustrate this famous individual where no free equivalent is available or could be created that would adequately provide the same image qualifies as fair use under United States copyright law.
4. Ishikawa, Kaoru, *What is Total Quality Control? the Japanese Way*, 1985, Prentice Hall, Englewood Cliffs, NJ
5. Main, Jeremy, Langan, Patricia A., August 18, 1986, "Under the Spell of the Quality Gurus" *Fortune Magazine*, pp. 22-23
6. http://www.shainin.com, retrieved May 4, 2011
7. National Institute of Standards and Technology: *NIST/SEMATECH e-Handbook of Statistical Methods*, http://www.itl.nist.gov/div898/handbook/section4/prc43.htm, May 4, 2011
8. Wikipedia.com, "Manufacturing resource planning," retrieved May 4, 2011
9. J.D. Edwards White Paper, http://www.sccori.com/SCM/COLLABORATIVEPLANNINGFORECASTING.pdf
10. L. Wylie, "A Vision of Next Generation MRP II", Scenario S-300-339, April 12, 1990, Gartner Group, Stamford, CT
11. Porter, Michael E., *Competitive Strategy: Techniques for Analyzing Industries and Competitors,* 1980, The Free Press, New York, NY
12. Helfert, Erich A., *Techniques of Financial Analysis*, 1967, Richard D. Irwin, Inc., Homewood, IL

Glossary

The terms in this glossary are used in typical business operations.

5	
5S Principles	Japanese words, , , , and 1. Sort (seiri – organize) 2. Straighten or simplify (seiton – arrange) 3. Sweep or scrub (seiso – clean) 4. Standardize (seiketsu – consistent organization / methods) 5. Self-discipline or sustain (shitsuke – make 5S a habit).
5 Whys	Find the root cause of problems by asking `why?' five times (or as often as necessary) for causes of causes.
14	
Deming's 14 Points	1. Create constancy of purpose 2. Adopt the new philosophy (of quality) 3. Cease dependence on mass inspection to achieve quality 4. End the practice of awarding business on the basis of price alone 5. Improve constantly and forever the system of production and service 6. Institute training on the job 7. Institute leadership 8. Drive out fear 9. Break down barriers between departments 10. Eliminate slogans, exhortations, and targets for the work force 11. Eliminate work standards on the factory floor and eliminate management by objectives as practiced 12. Remove barriers that rob employees of pride of workmanship 13. Institute a vigorous program of education and self-improvement 14. Put everybody to work to accomplish the transformation
A	
Absorption	Fixed costs are the costs of being in business, as opposed to the cost of doing business. Under normal circumstances, these costs continue at the same rate regardless of sales volume generated. Such costs are paid, like everything else, out of revenue and are conceptually absorbed by the goods and services produced. If fewer goods and services are produced,

	each unit will have to absorb more of the fixed costs.
Activity Based Costing (ABC)	An analytical accounting tool that assigns otherwise allocated costs to products / customers based directly on the resources used to produce / serve them.
Acid Test	An extreme version of the Current Ratio, the "Acid Test" assumes Inventory cannot be converted to cash.
Asset Leverage	Use of assets to gain the optimum revenue (measured as Revenue divided by Assets).
B	
Balance Sheet	Standard financial statement that presents assets, liabilities, and equity as of the end of one or more fiscal periods. This statement describes what is owned (assets) and who owns them (creditors, in the case of liabilities, or owners in the case of equity).
Balanced Scorecard	A system of metrics that summarizes significant data, ensuring executives are looking at customer needs, financial performance, efficiency, employee indicators, and investments in the future in a balanced way.
Benchmarking	The process of measuring products, services, and practices against those of leading companies.
Best-in-Class	A best-known example of performance in a particular operation. One needs to define both the class and the operation to avoid using the term loosely.
Breakeven	Breakeven Analysis involves computation of the point at which profit contribution (revenue minus variable cost) exactly equals the fixed costs of a company.
Breakthrough Objectives	Imaginative, stretch objectives providing significant competitive advantages and requiring significant change in an organization.
Brownfield	An existing and operating production facility.
Bottleneck	Anything that limits the throughput of a process.
Business Case	The justification for taking an action, especially when it involves making an investment. Focus is generally on the financial benefits, but non-financial benefits can also be important or even paramount.
Business Model	A description of how a company means to serve its customers, and earn money, including its strategy (what it will do) and its implementation concepts (how it will do it).
C	
Cannibalization	This occurs when a new product takes some of its market share from its owner's existing products, in effect cannibalizing other planned revenue.
Capitalization	Investments in systems, machinery and equipment, or people-

	related costs if their work results in an amortized asset (such as software).
Carrying Cost	Carrying Cost generally refers to the costs of "carrying" (holding) inventory, including the financial costs of (interest on) cash that is invested in inventory plus typical warehousing costs, often expressed as a per cent of inventory value.
Cash Flow / Funds Flow Statement	Standard financial statement that shows how cash was obtained and used in one or more fiscal periods.
Cells	Semi-autonomous and multi-skilled teams who manufacture complete products or complex components in one location.
Chaku-Chaku	A production line where the operator loads the part into the first machine and it is automatically passed from one machine to the next without operator involvement.
Champion	Key buyer/influencer who is the executive sponsor
Change Agent	An individual who sees and brings to reality a new way of doing business.
Changeover	The installation of a different tool, mold, die, or control program in a production machine (such as a lathe or milling machine, injection molding machine, or painting system).
Chart Of Accounts	A hierarchical numerical index of financial elements designed for sub-totaling financial transactions into meaningful categories.
Close	The concluding activities that finalize an agreement (usually signed) between a buyer and a seller. 'Close' is also used as a verb to indicate the seller's activity to secure a signed agreement.
Consolidation (of Businesses)	Consolidation refers to combining two or more business entities, taking into account their existing interactions to prevent certain transactions from being double-counted.
Constraint	Anything that limits a system from achieving higher performance or throughput.
Content	Written material pertaining to your company and / or product, presented in print or electronically via the web.
Contingency Planning	Planning for actions to mitigate risks.
Continuous Flow Production	Production where pieces are completed one at a time in a continuous sequence. Each process makes only the one piece that the next process needs, and the transfer batch size is one.
Continuous Improvement Process (CIP)	The never-ending process of improving quality and / or eliminating waste within an organization.
Control Chart	A statistical tool tracking a process to ensure it functions to produce output within established limits.

Control Element	A specific process variable which must be controlled in an experiment.
Counter measures	Immediate actions taken to bring performance that is tracking below expectations back into the proper trend.
Covariance	A measure of the strength of correlation between two or more random variables.
CRM	Customer Relationship Management – usually referring to software solutions supporting the sales and service processes
Currency Conversion	Translation of the value of one country's currency into another, using current or projected exchange rates.
Current Ratio	Current Assets divided by Current Liabilities, a measure of liquidity, or the ability to pay current debts out of current assets.
Current State Map	A schematic illustrating a current process.
Customer	A prospect that has purchased.
Cycle Time	The time required to complete one cycle of an operation.
D	
Daily Management	Attention each day to those issues concerned with the normal operation of a business.
Days Sales Outstanding (DSO)	A measure of Accounts Receivable, measured as A/R divided by annual Revenue, times 365. How many days we wait after delivering a product to get paid for it.
Days' supply of inventory	Total number of days (if the production level equals zero) that it would take to deplete finished goods inventory for the specified product line.
Debt / Equity Ratio	Total Liabilities divided by Total Equity, indicating the balance of the stakes held between owners and creditors.
Dependent Events	Events that occur only after a previous event.
Discount Rate	The rate of interest assumed to represent the current cost of money.
Discounted Cash Flow	An evaluation of a cash stream that devalues future cash flow in today's currency based on the time value of money concept.
Distribution Channel	The organizational path through which a business chooses to sell its products. Multiple channels are commonly used, such as direct sales through call centers or on the Internet, sales through retailers, resellers or VARs, and more.
Dividend Yield	The value of Dividends paid compared to the Market Value of a stock.
E	
EBITDA	(Earnings before Interest, Taxes, Depreciation, and Amortization) is a measure commonly used by investors to understand a company's ability to incur and service debt.
Economic Buyer	The key buyer/influencer in the sales cycle who holds the

	budget decision making power
EOQ (Economic Order Quantity)	EOQ is the right amount of an item to order to minimize the trade-off between ordering costs and the carrying cost of inventory.
Enterprise Software or Enterprise Resource Planning (ERP) Software	ERP systems or integrated Best of Breed systems with powerful middleware can support all of the communications needed for smooth operations throughout an organization. However, MRP (Manufacturing Resource Planning) systems that attempt to drive production may in fact be a barrier to lean, and build wasteful WIP (Work in Process) inventory.
Error Proofing	Designing a cause of potential failure, or a hazard to safety, out of a product or process.
F	
Fixed Cost	This refers to costs that don't change with changes in Revenue.
Financial Statements	Financial statements have evolved over the years to show in standard, easy to read format what a company owns and owes, whether it is making or losing money, and whether its cash flow is positive or negative. The three general forms of financial statements are: 1. Balance Sheet 2. Profit & Loss (P&L) also called the Income Statement 3. Cash Flow / Funds Flow Statement
Fiscal Year	The twelve month period, starting any month that a company uses to plan, budget, and report its business.
Flow	Movement of product continuously from raw material to finished goods through a production system that acted as one long conveyor.
Flow Chart	A schematic chart that illustrates a process, sometimes showing the 'as is' and 'to be' processes for comparison, identifying wasteful steps.
Flow Production	Production designed to pull product from operation to operation in the smallest increment (ideally one piece at a time).
Functional Layout	The practice of grouping machines or activities by type of operation performed.
Future State Map	A blueprint for a 'to be' process.
G	
Gain Sharing	An approach to providing incentives for team success, such as a share of the cost reduction or revenue increase.
Greenfield	A new production facility.
Gross Profit Margin	Gross Profit is the contribution made toward corporate expenses by the sale of products, calculated as a percentage: Revenue – Cost of Goods Sold / Revenue.

GTM	Go-to-Market, a strategy for market positioning
H	
High Performance Teams	Teams that perform complex tasks correctly and quickly.
Histogram	A chart that displays a series of metrics (x axis) according to the frequency of each (y axis) in order to understand variations. With enough data points this may result in a standard curve.
Reseller	Third party sales agent
Hosted	IT infrastructure provided by Managed Service Provider
Hurdle Rate	This refers to an organization's minimum rate of return required of all investments. If the estimated return falls below that rate, the investment will be rejected.
I	
Income Statement	Standard financial statement that presents revenue, costs, and the resulting profits for one or more fiscal periods. (Also called the P&L Statement.)
Insourcing and Outsourcing	Contract with an outside source to purchase goods or services previously produced in-house / produce in-house goods or services that were previously purchased outside.
Integrated Product Development	Refers to processes that bring engineering, marketing, financial, and production experts together to design and introduce new products.
Internal Growth Rate	The maximum growth rate achievable without external financing of any kind.
Internal Rate of Return (IRR)	Internal Rate of Return refers to the rate of return calculated directly from the cash outflows and inflows of that project.
Inventory	Inventory includes all raw materials, purchased parts, work-in-process, and finished goods not yet purchased. Consumable production supplies may also be accounted as inventory.
Inventory Turns	A measure of how often inventory is completely replenished in a given period (usually a year).
J	
Just-in-Time (JIT)	A system for producing and delivering the right items to the right place at the right time, in the right amounts. 'Just-in-Time' requires focus on balanced flow, pull procedures, standard work, and Takt time.
K	
Kaizen	Japanese for little fixes, generally applied to team efforts of a few days (Kaizen Blitz) to rapidly analyze and improve processes or sub- processes.
Kanban	A signaling device, often 'low tech,' which orders parts to be

	produced and delivered in a pull system.
KPI	Key Performance Indicators
L	
Lead	Any person or company that might be interested in your product or solution, but that has not yet been qualified.
Lead Time	The time a customer must wait for an order to be filled. This applies also to a process on a production line waiting for work pieces to arrive.
Lean	Business processes requiring less human effort, capital investment, floor space, materials, and time in all aspects of operation.
Life Cycle	Product life is measured from development, through sales growth and decline, to eventual exit and disposal.
Liquidity	Ease and speed with which an asset can be converted to cash.
M	
Marginal Tax Rate	Tax payable on the next taxable dollar earned.
Metrics	Analytics used to measure performance.
Mergers And Acquisitions	Business combinations involving purchases or stock swaps.
Mistake Proofing	Any equipment or procedure change to an operation that helps the operator reduce or eliminate errors.
MRP	Manufacturing Resource Planning – usually referring to large integrated production planning and control systems
Muda	Japanese for waste, applied to anything that interferes with the value stream.
Multi-Skilled Worker	Associates at any organizational level with diverse skills, providing flexibility in a production process.
N	
Net Present Value (NPV)	Net Present Value is a calculated estimate of the value of an investment's cash outflows and inflows over the life of the investment.
Non-Value Added	Activities that add no customer demanded value to a product or service.
One Piece Flow	Operators transfer each item individually to the next process step.
O	
Operating Cycle	The number of days from the time money is spent until it is collected, from the purchases that go into inventory to the collection of receivables.
Operating Expenses	The money required for the organization to be in the business, making product and supporting the operation.
Opportunity	A qualified lead with an interest and intent to purchase if

	justified.
Opportunity Costs	Opportunity Cost is the cost of NOT gaining an alternative financial benefit of an investment.
Other People's Money (OPM)	Funds raised from sources other than the owners. The term OPM is sometimes used to describe seed money provided by "Angels" or "Friends and Family" investors to start a new venture.
Out Of Pocket (OOP)	Out of Pocket costs are investment costs that require cash or cash equivalents.
Overall Equipment Effectiveness	OEE provides insights into the effectiveness of production equipment by measuring output versus capacity. This measure does not take into account any downtime explanations including such legitimate ones asas planned shutdowns
Overproduction	Producing more, sooner or faster than is required by the next process.
P	
Payback	A measure of how long until the income from an investment covers the cash outflow.
PDCA (Plan, Do, Check, Act)	A logical sequence for fixing any problem, unfortunately frequently forgotten. PLAN: Analyze the problem and develop an appropriate plan of action, specifying who, what, where, when, and how and the expected benefits. DO: Perform the actions. CHECK: Review the measurements to ensure benefits are on track. ACT: Redirect efforts as necessary.
Pareto Chart	A vertical bar graph showing the frequency of causes of error in descending order, generally indicating that a few causes are most frequent (the 80/20 rule).
Peer Group	Firms with similar assets, operations, and markets.
Perfection	An unattainable goal approached by optimizing value-added activities
Poka-Yoke	Error / mistake proofing using devices or procedures to prevent inefficient or unsafe actions. For examples, in-line weighing would prevent out of spec parts from proceeding to the next step, and safety gates would keep hands out of dangerous machines.
Price/Earnings (P/E) Ratio	The value of a stock expressed as a multiple of a company's earnings.
Price Sensitivity	Price usually has an impact on demand. Often when prices are reduced, the volume of goods sold increases. Higher prices may

	decrease the volume.
Pro Forma Financial Statement	a financial statement which projects future years' operations
Process	Operations that transform material (or paperwork) from input to finished product.
Process Reengineering	Integrated restructuring of operations to improve effectiveness and efficiency.
Process Map	A visual representation of the sequential flow of a process to identify opportunities for improvement.
Processing Time	The time a product is actually being worked on in a machine or work area
Profit & Loss (P&L) Statement	Standard financial statement that presents revenue, costs, and the resulting profits for one or more fiscal periods. (Also called the Income Statement.)
Profit Margin	Profit Margin is a percentage calculated as Net Profit after Tax divided by Revenue.
Prospect	An individual or an organization that appears ready to buy and represents a selling opportunity.
Pull	A system of cascading production and delivery instructions from downstream to upstream activities in which the upstream supplier waits until the downstream customer signals a need.
Pull System	Product is pulled through a process, starting with the end user. A sale triggers production of another unit, production of the unit triggers suppliers to send sub-assemblies or raw materials, and so on. Very little excess inventory is created.
Push System	Product is pushed into a process, regardless of whether it is needed, often creating excess inventory.
Q	
Qualification	A vetting process, and term used in sales referring to confirmation that a lead is interested and intends to purchase.
Quality Function Deployment (QFD)	A visual decision-making tool for cross-functional project teams that focuses on the voice of the customer, addresses product performance targets and trade-offs, and develops consensus and team commitment to product specifications. QFD reduces expensive rework as projects near launch.
Quality Management	The organizations, practices, and tools that make it possible to plan, manufacture, and deliver quality products / services.
Quick Changeover	Rapid change of tooling / fixtures when multiple products run on the same machine.
Queue Time	The time a product spends in a line awaiting the next design, order processing, or fabrication step.
R	

RACI	Responsible-Accountable-Consulted-Informed – descriptions of Roles and Responsibilities, to be analyzed and clarified as needed
Reengineering	Fundamentally revising integrated processes throughout a company to improve quality and efficiently.
Resource Utilization	Using a resource for any purpose (preferably to add value).
ROI (Return On Investment)	Whenever an investment is made, the investor needs to understand when and how it will be recovered and how much it will eventually return.
ROI-Driven Sales Process	A method of selling which reinforces value and building a comprehensive business case with financial metrics
ROIC (Return On Invested Capital)	After-tax earnings on the average assets employed, a useful measure of investment quality
S	
SaaS	Software as a Service
Sales Channel	Multiple paths for selling to distribution points
Sales Playbook	Sales best practices formatted for easy reference.
Sales Process	The activity conducted by sales organizations to build value, demonstrate ROI, and close sales.
Sensei	A master / teacher who helps implement lean or Six Sigma practices. The term was originally applied in Oriental martial arts.
Sequential Changeover	Changeover / setup of machines within Takt time so that multiple products can be made on the same line without interrupting the flow.
Scenario Analysis	An analysis based on a specific set of conditions. Generally several scenarios will be generated to compare the effects of "what if" situations.
Sensitivity Analysis	Analysis of the effect that a single variable has on the ROI of an investment.
Shareholder Value	The market value of a company's stock divided by the book value of the company, representing the premium stock purchasers are willing to pay for the assets of the company under its current management.
Single Minute Exchange of Dies (SMED)	Concept of rapid machine changeover / setup to keep production flowing with minimal downtime when multiple products run on the same machine. Ideally changeover would be instantaneous and would not interfere with continuous flow.
Single-Piece Flow	A production process in which products are pulled through production one complete product at a time.
SMB	Small and mid-size businesses, generally less than $1 billion in annual revenues

Glossary

Social Media	Formats for interaction among people and businesses usually conducted via the web, in which they create and exchange information and ideas.
Standards	Accepted norms, often set by regulatory organizations.
Standard Work	A precise description of each work activity specifying cycle time, Takt time, the work sequence of specific tasks, and the minimum inventory of parts on hand needed to conduct the activity.
Standard Work in Process	The minimum amount of material for a given product which must be in process at any time to ensure proper flow of the operation.
Sunk Cost	A sunk cost is a cost already incurred (paid or obligated), and therefore not relevant to an investment decision.
Standardization	Use of uniform methods and processes to ensure uniform output
Supplier Partnership	Close working relationship with a supplier to gain mutual benefits, such as more revenue or less cost through better designs, logistics, etc.
Supply Chain	The path materials take to move from raw materials through processes in multiple business entities to reach the final product
Sustainable Growth Rate	The maximum growth rate achievable maintaining a constant debt-equity ratio without external equity financing.
Sub-Optimization	Taking action to improve efficiency in one area that negatively impacts the efficiency of another area even more.
Suspects	Any entities that appear on a marketing list, generally comprised of target market organizations.
T	
Takt Time	The available production time divided by the rate of customer demand. For example, if customers demand 480 automobiles per 480 minute shift, Takt time is one minute.
Theory of Constraints	A lean management philosophy focused on removing constraints to increase throughput and decrease inventory / expenses.
Throughput Time	The time required by a process to complete its value-adding activities.
Total Productive Maintenance (TPM)	A disciplined integration of maintenance schedules with production schedules in order to prevent unplanned down time and gain optimum run time from every significant machine.
Toyota Production System (TPS)	A manufacturing philosophy that relentlessly attacks waste while improving quality and shortening work cycles
Trusted Advisor	An individual who has established credibility through ideas offered and honorable dealings.
V	
Value	The right product (defined by the customer) at the right price

	(defined by the competition).
Value-Added Analysis	Analysis of activities to determine which add value from the customer's perspective in order to eliminate non-value adding activities (wasted effort).
Value-Added Reseller (VAR)	An outside sales agent who bundles your product or solution into his or her more robust product or solution.
Value Proposition	Proof statements showing financial gains that a product purchase will provide
Value Stream / Value Chain	The progressive sequential activities that add value to a product –material management, fabrication, logistics, etc. – from raw material to finished product.
Value Stream Mapping	Creating a schematic of how material gains value as it moves through an operation in order to identify opportunities to eliminate waste.
Variable Cost	Cost that varies directly with the number of units produced.
Vertical Teams	Teams that include employees from multiple organizational levels.
Vision	A long-term view of what the company is and aspires to in terms of its business model, systems for management, and processes.
Visual Control	Information, parts, and tools displayed for instant understanding of the process or system status.
Voice of the Customer (VOC)	Establishing product /service designs and features based on carefully listening to what the customer wants and needs.
W	
Waste	Anything produced that has no value; any use of resources that produces nothing of value.
Work in Progress (WIP)	Product or inventory in various stages of completion throughout the plant, once released as raw material to the floor and before becoming finished goods ready for shipment.
Work Sequence	The order in which work steps occur.
Working Capital	The funds invested to support day to day operations of a business.
World Class	An overused term meaning 'done as well as the best in the world.'
Y	
Yield	Per cent of material and labor input that becomes acceptable finished product.
Z	
Zero-Based Budgeting	A budget built from scratch, replacing justification based on historical spending with justification based on requirements of current value-adding activities.

Glossary